Projects in CDT

John Peace

with illustrations by John Dimond

HODDER AND STOUGHTON
LONDON AUCKLAND SYDNEY TORONTO

KT-179-007

Preface

Having worked for many years in industry the author first envisaged the book whilst teaching students on EITB courses at Further Education Colleges. The concept and style of the book developed over a number of years with many of the projects being designed and made by pupils at Stoke Park Comprehensive School in Coventry where the author was responsible for developing technology courses for the lower school.

One aim of this book is to provide ideas which could assist pupils to develop their own briefs. The book does *not* set out to provide all the theory needed to carry out projects listed. Pupils would research projects as an integral part of their technological design process.

The projects shown on the contents page have been designed to include the technological areas of Energy, Mechanisms, Structures, Materials and Electrics. Opinions of their importance could well influence the way the projects are solved.

It is not possible to categorise closely each project by age, ability or content. Therefore each project is introduced at a level which, at its simplest, enables the project to be built by the least able pupil and will stand on its own right as a job, thus ensuring that *all* pupils achieve success at some level. Equally, for more able and experienced pupils, progressively more demanding problems are posed. The teachers will find this range of 'starter' projects invaluable for enthusing their class into participation.

Peace, J.
   Projects in CDT
   1. Secondary schools. Curriculum subjects:
   Crafts, design & technology. Projects –
   For teaching
   I. Title   II. Dimond J
   607'.2

ISBN 0 340 41146 5

First published 1988

Printed in Great Britain
for Hodder and Stoughton Educational
a division of Hodder and Stoughton Ltd, Mill Road,
Dunton Green, Sevenoaks, Kent by

St Edmundsbury Press Ltd,
Bury St Edmunds, Suffolk.
Photoset by Rowland Phototypesetting Ltd,
Bury St Edmunds, Suffolk.

CONTENTS

INTRODUCTION

Technology is essentially the process by which people cope with their environment. It is therefore a problem-solving and making activity rather than a body of knowledge. It is a design activity operating within recognised constraints and available resources.

The purpose of this book is not to introduce technological content, but to provide stimulus and experience of technologically based problem-solving activities. In balanced CDT courses for the middle or lower secondary age range, there is a great need for technology projects as part of this balance. A technology project is therefore a means of engaging pupils in this process at a level appropriate to their age, experience, knowledge and ability.

This book assumes an age range of 9 to 14 years. The approach to each subject is such that an introduction is given in each section (where appropriate). The suggested briefs become progressively more sophisticated, and almost any topic can be undertaken at the level of the pupil in question.

Many pupils find difficulty in identifying situations within which technological problem-solving can take place. This publication will therefore provide *ideas* for pupils and resource material for teachers. The aim is to allow the pupil to select a project from the book, develop it through and *improve* upon it, with limited guidance from the teacher, i.e. pupil experiences will follow on from the introduction of technological concepts.

Projects are shown using easily available 'components'. Plastic containers by virtue of their shape, design and material properties lend themselves readily to building projects successfully and quickly. Time saved in not having to build structures continually allows for greater concentration on technological concepts of CDT studies in this age range.

Acknowledgements

I would like to thank the following people for their help in the preparation of this book:

David Shaw, who recognised that I may have something to offer my fellow colleagues, for encouraging me to put it into print and for subsequent assistance in editing and photographing the projects involved; Christine Dimond, for typing the manuscript; my wife Ann and my sons Gary and Michael; who provided the inspiration to continue with the book and assisted in the manufacture, improvement and testing of many of the projects involved; John Scott-Scott, an indispensable catalyst in the development of ideas; the pupils of Stoke Park Comprehensive School and The Junior School of Brighton College.

WATER ROCKET

Introduction

Everyone has at some time blown up a balloon (Fig. 1) and let it go. It shoots away and tends to whirl about until there is no air left in it and then it falls to the ground. It is the air rushing out of the balloon's 'mouth' that forces the balloon to move in the opposite direction.

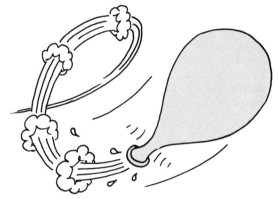

Fig. 1 Blow up the balloon and let it go!

Fig. 2 Control!

By pinching the mouth of the balloon (Fig. 2) you can get it to make a screeching noise as the air comes out. In fact you have *controlled* the amount of air being released. Knowing this, and using the following information, you can design your own squeezy (washing-up liquid) bottle rocket powered by air and water. *Amaze* your friends by stating how far it will go.

SAFETY NOTE

Wear goggles in case the bottle bursts!

How it works (Photo 1)

Half-fill your squeezy-bottle rocket with water, then push a car tyre valve (schrader valve) into the mouth (see Figure 3). Blow up (*pressurise*) your rocket using a car footpump (Figure 4 shows one way of doing this). When the pressure inside is great enough, the rocket will

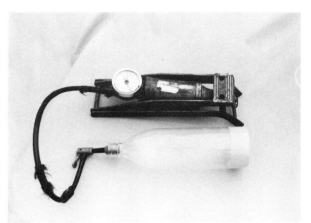

Photo 1

be blown off the valve, and, as the water is forced out, fired upwards to a height of 10 metres. See Figure 5.

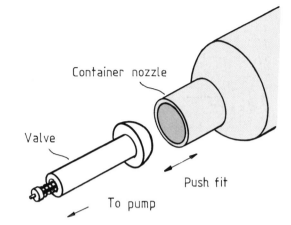

Container nozzle

Valve

Push fit

To pump

Fig. 3

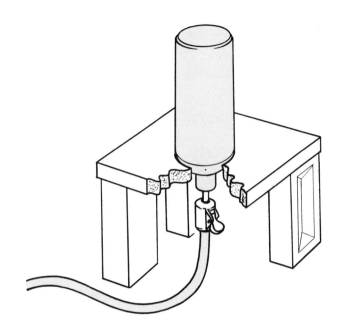

Fig. 4

BANG

Fig. 5

NOTE

You may have to cut the schrader valve to fit the neck of the bottle. With practice you will soon find the right fit. Wrapping tape or cloth around the valve (Fig. 6) will help you to do this.

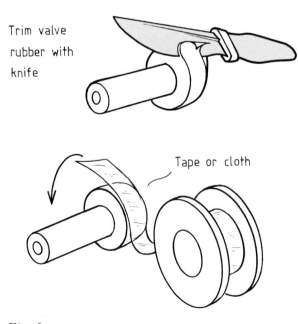

Trim valve rubber with knife

Tape or cloth

Fig. 6

Brief 1.1

Design a water rocket, using a plastic squeezy bottle as the body shell, to travel as far as possible (Photo 2).

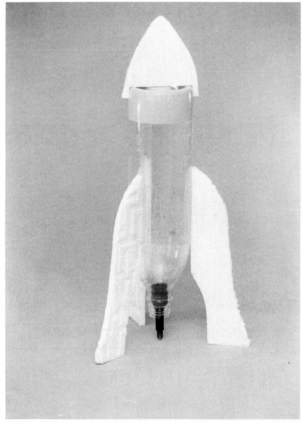

Photo 2

Why does a racing car travel faster than a bus? One reason is that the racing car is streamlined. That is, it offers less resistance to the air when travelling along the road (Figures 7 and 8).

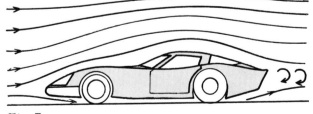

Fig. 7

How can you alter the shape of your squeezy-bottle rocket to make it more streamlined?.

AIRFLOW ⟶

Fig. 8

Things to do and to find out

1 Fit a cone to the nose of the bottle. Does it go further?

2 What effect does fitting wings have on your bottle?

3 Does the fitting of fins make any difference?

4 Does the bottle still work equally well with all the extra weight?

5 How could you fit improvements to your bottle rocket?

6 What would happen if you fitted a flat piece of card to the front of your bottle? Try it.

Brief 1.2

Design a launch pad for your squeezy-bottle rocket.

If you launch a rocket on bonfire night it is usually placed in a milk bottle or another suitable launching pad (Fig. 9). If you did not do this, the rocket would not launch well or travel in the desired direction. The rocket needs a support (structure) of some sort, so that you can *control* the direction of its movement through the air.

You have also seen ski-jumpers who use a launching ramp to enable themselves to travel

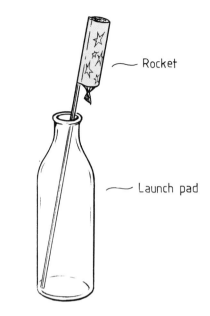

Fig. 9

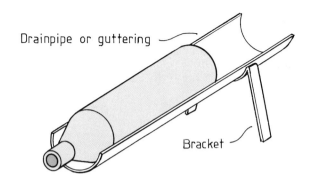

Fig. 11

Fig. 10

Things to do and to find out

1 How many ways can you think of to adjust the pad? Sketch them.

2 What are the best materials to use for your launch pad?

3 What happens to the rocket when you alter the angle of the launch pad?

4 What angle produces the greatest flight distance?

5 Does the length of the launch pad slipway affect the rocket's performance?

6 Does oiling (lubricating) the slipway increase the distance travelled by the rocket?

Brief 1.3

Design a rocket-powered cable car (Photo 3).

Photo 3

through the air (Fig. 10). The winner is the one who jumps the furthest. These skiers use a hard slippery surface to go faster – they are reducing the *friction* between the skis and the ground.

Can you design an adjustable launch pad for your squeezy-bottle rocket that will help you control the distance travelled? One example is shown in Figure 11. Remember! You must choose materials that will help you reduce friction.

Cable cars and ski lifts travel along a steel wire. Aerial runways are used to take people from higher to lower ground quickly. In each case a vehicle or person is suspended from the wire.

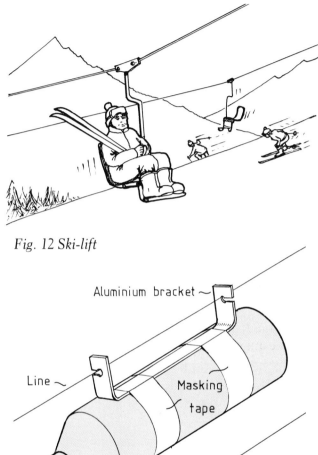

Fig. 12 Ski-lift

Fig. 13

Stretch some string or wire between two posts 10 metres apart. Hang your cable car from the wire using a device similar to those shown in Figure 13. Remember: this device

must be able to slide easily along the wire, so it must be smooth and hard. Make sure the line is as tight as possible. Lower one end of the line until the rocket just starts to slide.

If you use string, you may find that rubbing it with candle wax reduces the *friction*. Friction occurs between two surfaces moving against one another. Try rubbing your hands together. They get hot and more difficult to move. This is because of friction.

Things to do and to find out

1 Why is there no point in putting water into the bottle in this case?

2 What is the best material for the hooks?

3 Does streamlining the cable car improve the length of the run? – or its speed?

4 Do more hooks improve the performance?

5 Does the position of the hooks make any difference?

6 Repeat the experiment of fitting various shapes to the front of the rocket.

7 How does adding weight affect the performance of the rocket?

Brief 1.4

Design a water rocket to fire a tracer wire across a 10 metre span.

A tracer wire is a thin, light wire that is carried by a rocket across a gap or ravine. Its other end is attached to a stronger line, which can then be used to transport heavy objects such as people.

For the fireman to be able to save the person trapped by fire, he must shoot the tracer wire from a rocket at just the right angle for the victim to be able to catch it (Fig. 14). If the angle is too great, the tracer will go too high and not reach the victim. If it is too small, the tracer will hit the wall below the victim.

Can you adapt your rocket to carry a tracer wire across a 10-metre span?

Fig. 14

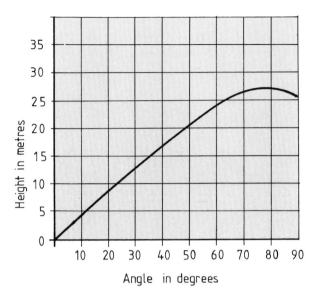

Fig. 15

We can alter the distance a water rocket travels by changing the angle, the amount of water content and the fit of the valve. We are able to control the distance travelled by knowing what happens when each of these items (*variables*) is changed. If we use a table or graph, we can plot the results. The diagram (Fig. 15) shows how this can be done, with height gained plotted against angle set.

Things to do and to find out

1 How will the tracer be attached to the rocket?

2 What is the best type of line to use as a tracer?

3 How will the tracer wire be paid out?

4 How strong must the tracer be?

5 How long will the line need to be?

6 What effects does weight have on the performance of the rocket?

Brief 1.5

Present some variables affecting the performance of a water rocket.

Things to do and to find out

1 Can you show the results obtained on a bar chart?

2 Are you able to plot two or more sets of results on the same graph?

3 Vary the angle of the launching pad and show the results.

4 What happens to the rocket if the water content is varied?

5 Compare the angle for the greatest height against the greatest distance. Explain any changes.

6 Can you think of other variables to affect the rocket's performance?

SIMPLE PROPELLER

Introduction

Propellers have many uses. They can be used to push or pull an aeroplane through the air and lift or slow the rate of descent of a helicopter (Figs 1 and 2). In water they can move a boat forwards or backwards (Fig. 3). They are even used to blow cold or hot air, as in a fan or a hair dryer.

Boat propeller

Fig. 3

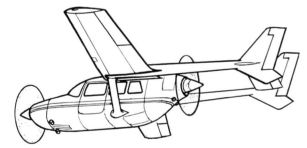

Fig. 1

Nature provides a natural propeller in the form of a sycamore seed (Fig. 4). The wings on a pair of seeds cause them to spin and fall slowly, allowing the air to carry the seeds away.

Sycamore seed

Fig. 2

Fig. 4

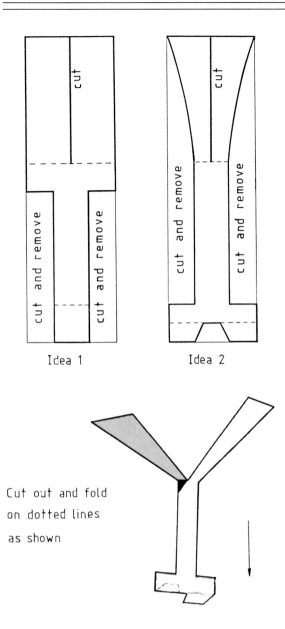

Idea 1   Idea 2

Cut out and fold
on dotted lines
as shown

Fig. 5

Figure 5 shows a sycamore seed 'look-alike' and, using this idea from nature, you can make your own. Cut one out and try it.

Things to do and to find out

1 Bend the wings in the other direction. Does the propeller spin (rotate) in the same way?

2 Alter the angle of the wings to get your propeller to fall (a) quickly, (b) slowly.

3 Colour the blades to make your propeller look better when it is spinning.

4 Does adding a small weight to the bottom of the propeller change its performance?

5 Make the biggest propeller you can out of some other material such as cardboard.

6 Can you get your propeller to fall into a circle of 150 mm diameter from a height of 3 metres?

7 Try dropping your model upside-down, as in Figure 6. The result may surprise you.

Try this way

Fig. 6

Brief 2.1

Construct a two-bladed propeller (Photo 1).

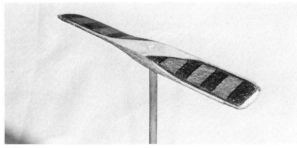

Photo 1

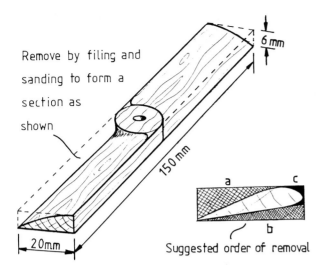

Remove by filing and sanding to form a section as shown

6 mm

150 mm

20mm

a   c

b

Suggested order of removal

Fig. 7

Fig. 9

When the blade of the propeller in Figures 7 and 8 spins fast enough, it will gain height. This is because the shape of the blades and the speed of it spinning has created *lift*. If an aeroplane can move through the air fast enough, the shape of the wings (cross-section, as in Figure 7) also creates this lift.

Hold a piece of paper at two corners and blow over the top of it. The paper rises, the blowing (increased air speed) causes a decrease in pressure on the top of the paper, the higher pressure underneath pushes the paper up – creating lift (Fig. 9).

When making the propeller, try to make sure that both sides are of the same thickness and length, otherwise it may not work well, because it will be out of balance.

When the shaping of the upper blades is completed, turn them over and repeat the process. Drill a Ø 6 mm (Ø means diameter) hole through the centre and ensure the dowel is a tight fit. A dense material such as mahogany will give better results.

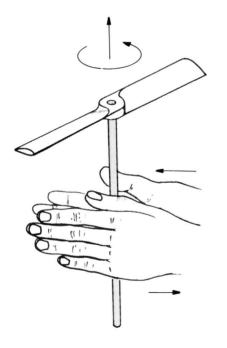

Fig. 8

Things to do and to find out

1 How can you check the balance of the propeller blades?

2 Does the direction in which you spin it make any difference?

3 Try a different material for your propeller, e.g. a thermoplastic sheet can be heated and bent.

4 What difference does the length of rod make to your propeller?

5 Colour your blades to make them show up more clearly when they are rotating.

Brief 2.2

Design a handle to enable the propeller to be launched using string as a means of rotation (Photo 2).

Photo 2

Drill hole ⌀6·8mm

30

30

10 +

30

Sketch assumes material is wood (20mm thick)

Fig. 10

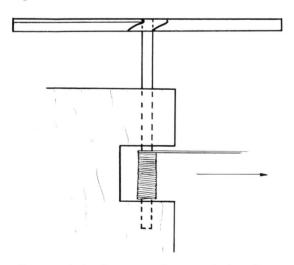

Ensure string is wrapped around stem in the correct direction, pull sharply and the propeller should rise 15metres or more.

Fig. 11

The sizes given in Figure 10 are known to work, but a comfortable grip needs to be designed into the handle to suit your hand size. Carefully drill the 6.8 mm diameter hole for alignment (accuracy). Wind some string around the stem (Fig. 11) and pull!

Better results will be achieved if you rub the stem with candle wax to reduce friction. (Rub your hands together hard and you will see what is meant by friction.)

Things to do and to find out

1 Wind the string in the other direction and note what happens.

2 Does a slot of more than 30 mm have any effect on your propeller?

3 Include some colour as a means of enhancing the look of your handle.

4 Can you make your propeller travel *further* over the ground than higher above it?

Brief 2.3

Design and build a two-bladed propeller to achieve the greatest possible height.

Why do some aeroplanes have different-shaped propeller blades? One reason is to make the best use of their available engine power. Why do ships have such coarse, large blades? It depends upon their size and weight, and the speed that they have to travel.

Things to do and to find out

1 Vary the blade angles as in Figure 12.

2 Change the material of the propeller.

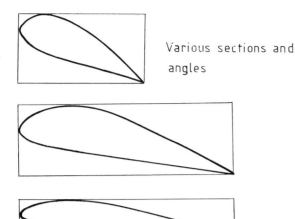

Various sections and angles

Fig. 12

3 Alter the blade lengths and widths and record performance changes.

4 How can you measure the height achieved by your propeller?

5 Carry out research to see where different blades are used and why.

Brief 2.4

Design a multi-bladed propeller.

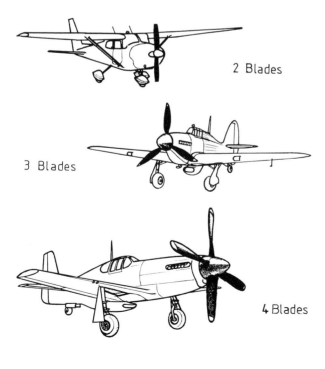

2 Blades

3 Blades

4 Blades

5 Blades

Fig. 13

Aeroplanes were built using two, three, four and five blades on each propeller (Fig. 13). Why do aeroplanes use a different number of blades?

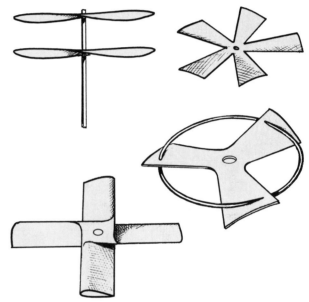

Fig. 14

Using the sketches in Figure 14 design a propeller with more than two blades. Prove by experiment which is better: two blades or more.

Things to do and to find out

1 Use different materials for your propeller, i.e. wood, plastics or metal.

2 Make a propeller using Figure 7 as a guide.

3 Does the smoothness of the blades' surface change their performance?

4 Add weights to the tips of the blades. How does this alter the performance?

5 Do more blades make your propeller go higher or further?

6 Tabulate the results of your investigations to show the best idea.

Brief 2.5

Given a propeller, design and build a helicopter powered by an elastic band(s).

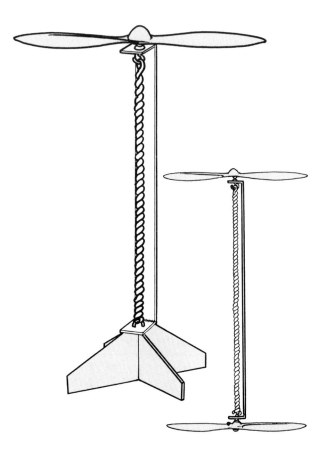

Fig. 15

Helicopters are lifted off the ground by a large rotor similar to a propeller. A tail rotor is added to stop the helicopter itself from spinning. You will need something on this helicopter to stop it spinning as well. In Figure 15, 'fins' have been added to ensure it remains stable and balanced and does not twist when released.

The body can have many shapes, but it must be light and strong.

NOTE

A factory-made propeller will help ensure success, as it is difficult to obtain the correct angles when making your own.

Things to do and to find out

1 How many fins are needed to stop the helicopter spinning?

2 What size will they have to be?

3 Try varying the propellers – this can be done by buying different types from a model shop.

4 Vary the length of the body.

5 Change the thickness of the rubber band and explain the changes.

6 Add a further propeller to the bottom of your helicopter.

7 Try using different materials for the helicopter's body. Remember – lightest is best!

ROTARY TO LINEAR

Introduction

Ever since cave people moved out of their caves, they needed an easy way to transport loads that were too heavy to carry. They developed the wheel (Fig. 1).

Today the world is full of different types of vehicles, and children of all ages love playing with models of them. Using everyday household containers here is an easy to make fun toy called a Movealong (Fig. 2). The things that you may need to build one are shown in Figs 3 to 8.

Fig. 2 Movealong

How to make your Movealong (Photo 1)

Fig. 1

Photo 1

You can use either half

Use two large beads
or
ping pong balls

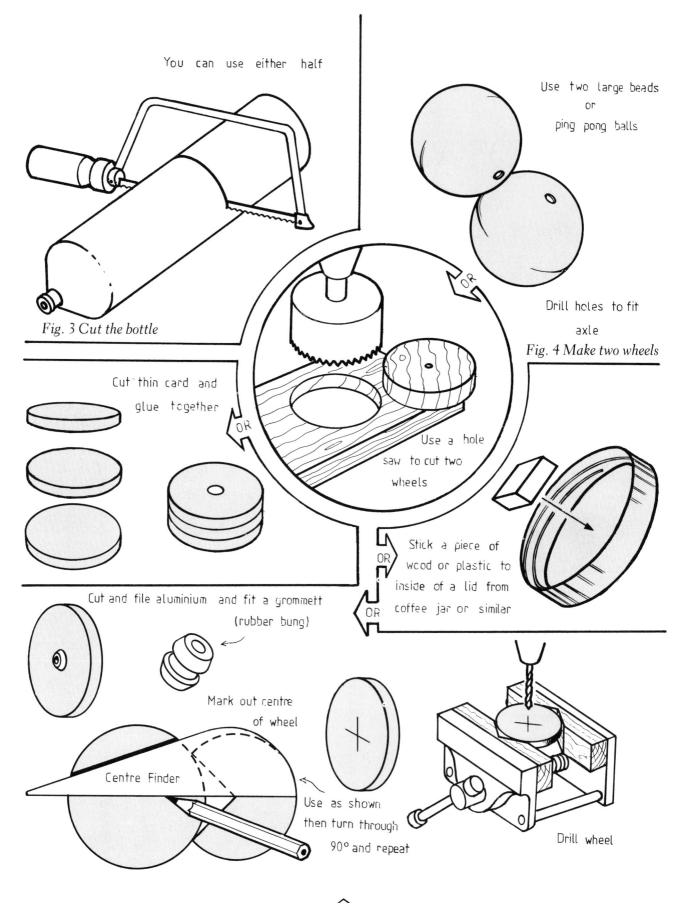

Fig. 3 Cut the bottle

Drill holes to fit
axle
Fig. 4 Make two wheels

Cut thin card and
glue together

OR

Use a hole
saw to cut two
wheels

OR   Stick a piece of
wood or plastic to
inside of a lid from
OR   coffee jar or similar

Cut and file aluminium and fit a grommett
(rubber bung)

Mark out centre
of wheel

Centre Finder

Use as shown
then turn through
90° and repeat

Drill wheel

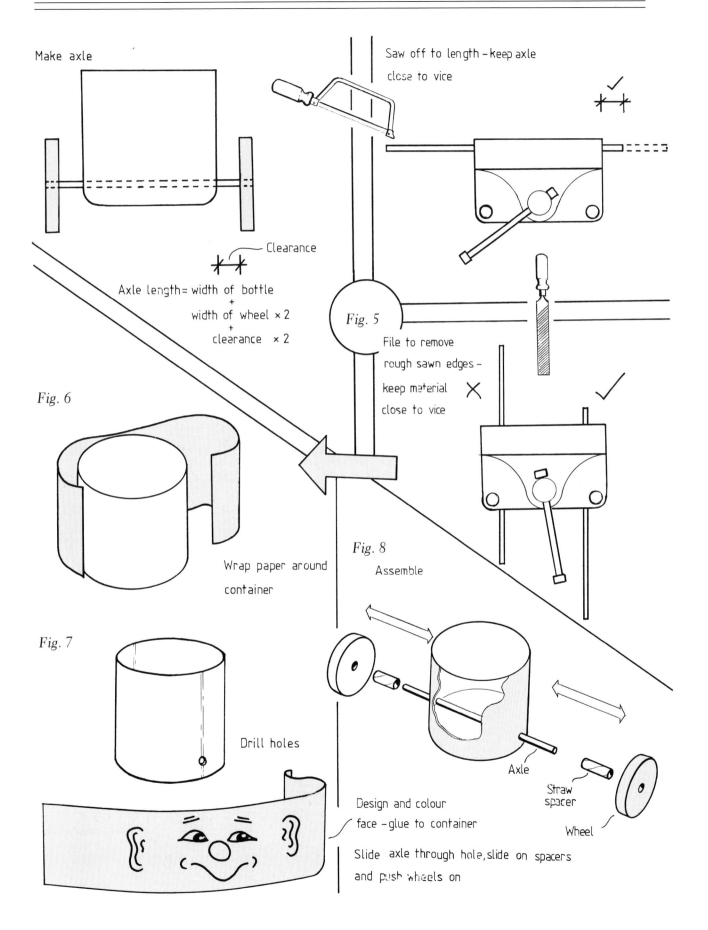

Make axle

Saw off to length – keep axle
close to vice

Clearance

Axle length = width of bottle
+
width of wheel × 2
+
clearance × 2

Fig. 5

File to remove
rough sawn edges –
keep material
close to vice

Fig. 6

Wrap paper around
container

Fig. 8

Assemble

Fig. 7

Drill holes

Design and colour
face – glue to container

Slide axle through hole, slide on spacers
and push wheels on

Axle

Straw
spacer

Wheel

1 Cut the squeezy bottle in half with a hacksaw blade or modelling knife to make the body shell (structure) (Fig. 3).

2 Make two wheels (Fig. 4).

3 Cut the axle to the correct length (Fig. 5).

4 Wrap paper around the body and cut it to size (Fig. 6).

5 Mark out and drill holes in bottle structure (Fig. 7).

6 Colour a face on paper.

7 Put the parts together (Fig. 8).

Brief 3.1

Design a toy, with an up-and-down motion, using a plastic bottle (Photo 2).

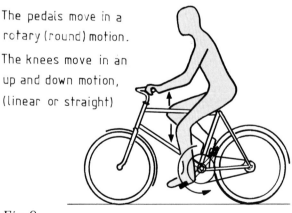

Photo 2

The pedals move in a rotary (round) motion.

The knees move in an up and down motion, (linear or straight)

Fig. 9

As the bicycle travels along the cyclist is using his legs to turn the pedals. Can you see that the pedals rotate – yet his knees move up and down? The pedals are on a shaft that has

been bent at right angles to form a *crank* (Figure 9). You are going to make a crank to change rotary movement into a straight-line (linear) movement (motion), as in Figure 10.

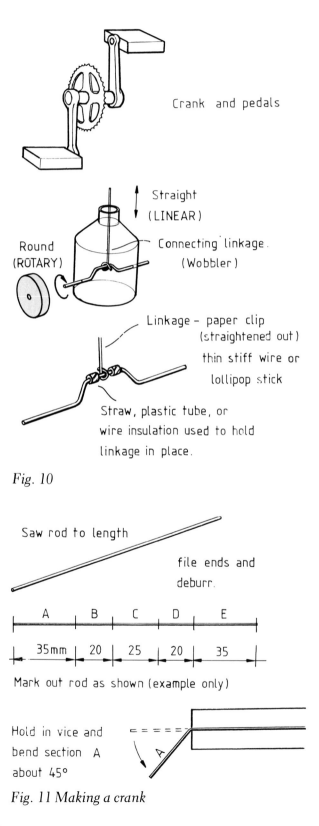

Crank and pedals

Straight (LINEAR)

Round (ROTARY)

Connecting linkage. (Wobbler)

Linkage – paper clip (straightened out)

thin stiff wire or lollipop stick

Straw, plastic tube, or wire insulation used to hold linkage in place.

Fig. 10

Saw rod to length

file ends and deburr.

A	B	C	D	E
35mm	20	25	20	35

Mark out rod as shown (example only)

Hold in vice and bend section A about 45°

Fig. 11 *Making a crank*

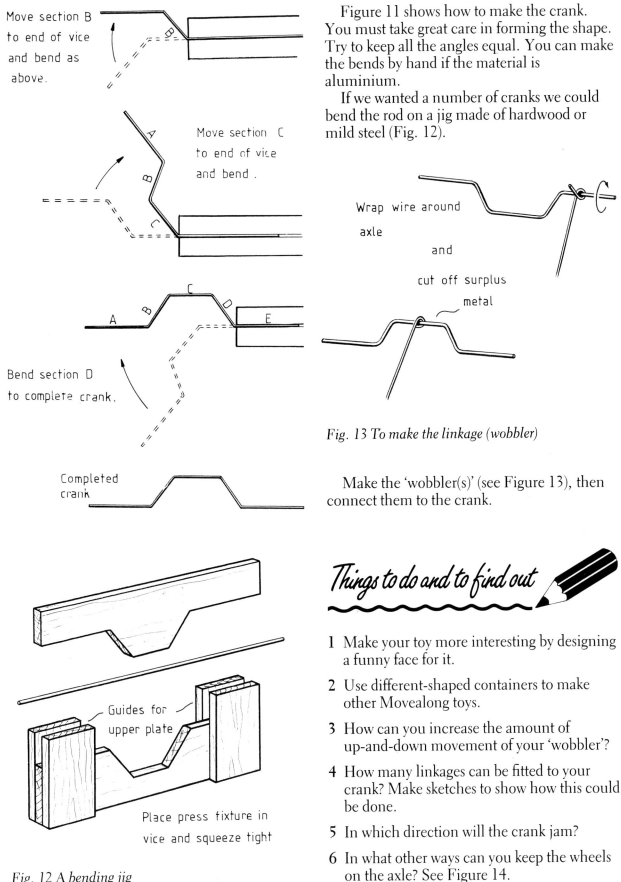

Move section B to end of vice and bend as above.

Move section C to end of vice and bend.

Bend section D to complete crank.

Completed crank

Figure 11 shows how to make the crank. You must take great care in forming the shape. Try to keep all the angles equal. You can make the bends by hand if the material is aluminium.

If we wanted a number of cranks we could bend the rod on a jig made of hardwood or mild steel (Fig. 12).

Wrap wire around axle and cut off surplus metal

Fig. 13 To make the linkage (wobbler)

Make the 'wobbler(s)' (see Figure 13), then connect them to the crank.

Guides for upper plate

Place press fixture in vice and squeeze tight

Fig. 12 A bending jig

Things to do and to find out

1 Make your toy more interesting by designing a funny face for it.

2 Use different-shaped containers to make other Movealong toys.

3 How can you increase the amount of up-and-down movement of your 'wobbler'?

4 How many linkages can be fitted to your crank? Make sketches to show how this could be done.

5 In which direction will the crank jam?

6 In what other ways can you keep the wheels on the axle? See Figure 14.

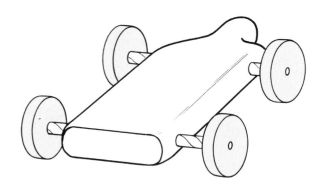

Fig. 16

If wood – drill holes in wheel slightly smaller than axle ∅ to make a tight fit.

If axle protrudes, drill a small hole and push paper clip through

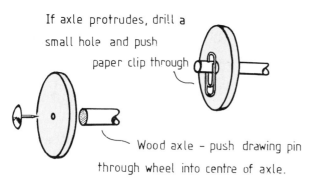

Wood axle – push drawing pin through wheel into centre of axle.

Knitting needles have small plastic caps that fit on ends – to fit size of needle.

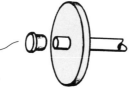

Fig. 14 How to keep wheels on

From the different-shaped plastic containers used in the home, you can make a really interesting four-wheeled toy (Figs 15 and 16). This will be better balanced (more stable) than the two-wheeled toy and travel further when pushed. Two or more wheels can be added to your present toy, or you can start again and design a new one.

Things to do and to find out

1 How can you make sure all four wheels touch the ground at the same time?

2 With Figure 15, how can you make the chassis?

3 With Figure 16, where can you fit the crank and how?

4 With Figure 16, where will the linkage go?

5 How can you stop the wheels rubbing against the body?

6 Decorate your toy to make it more attractive with either coloured PVC tape or acrylic paints.

Brief 3.2

Make a four-wheel toy from plastic bottles or other materials.

Brief 3.3

Using a rubber band, make your vehicle self-propelled.

Fig. 15

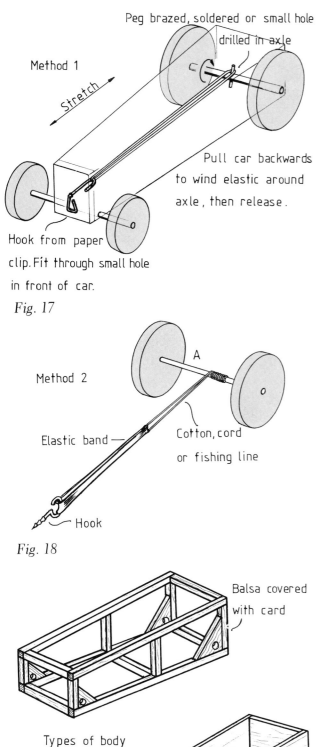

Method 1

Peg brazed, soldered or small hole drilled in axle

Stretch

Pull car backwards to wind elastic around axle, then release.

Hook from paper clip. Fit through small hole in front of car.

Fig. 17

Method 2

A

Elastic band

Cotton, cord or fishing line

Hook

Fig. 18

Balsa covered with card

Types of body

Plywood

Fig. 19

You can now improve your vehicle still further and get it to move under its own power (Figs 17 and 18). Or you can redesign a new body shape (structure) (Fig. 19). When this is completed, turn to Brief 8.3 to see how to use the energy stored in a rubber band!

Things to do and to find out

1 Which material is best for making your vehicle?

2 Devise other ways of fixing the hook for the elastic band at the front of the vehicle.

3 What other ways could you use to attach the other end of the elastic band to the rear axle?

4 What effect does the 'weight' of the material have on your vehicle?

5 Streamline your vehicle by using card and glue.

6 What effect does changing the size of the rear wheels have on your vehicle?

7 Vary the thickness of the elastic band and list the effects this has on your vehicle's performance.

Brief 3.4

Fit an electric motor to your vehicle (Photo 3).

Photo 3

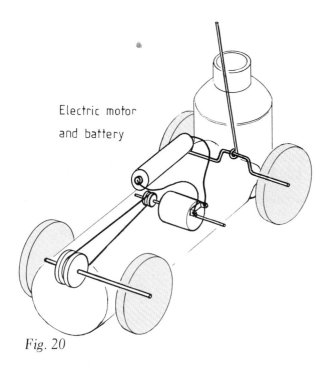

Electric motor
and battery

Fig. 20

Here is one way of powering your vehicle using a small electric motor and elastic bands (Fig. 20). You will need to experiment to mount the motor in the best position. If you are not sure how to build a simple circuit, see section 5 on lamps.

Things to do and to find out

1 What happens if the drive band is too tight or too loose?

2 What happens if you use a bigger pulley on the axle?

3 How can the battery be fitted?

4 What difference does the thickness of the rubber band make?

5 How fast does the toy travel? How will you measure this?

6 Design the toy to include some linkage movement.

7 Try to make it go as fast as possible.

8 Try to make it go as slowly as possible.

9 Try to make it go up the steepest slope possible.

10 What do you need to do to make 8 and 9 happen?

RUBBER-POWERED MOTOR

Introduction

Make a rubber-powered Rollalong (Photo 1).

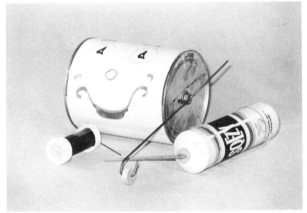

Photo 1

Rubber-powered motors come in many forms. With this easy-to-build one, a twisted band is used to provide the energy for it to move forwards or backwards (Fig. 1).

How it works

The lever (long rod) is used to wind up the elastic band, inside the Rollalong's body. The band now has energy stored in it (potential energy). Put the Rollalong on the ground and let go of the lever. The band will slowly unwind (releasing the energy) and the Rollalong will move.

NOTE

All the items needed to build the Rollalong can usually be found around the house.

How to make a Rollalong

To build (assemble) your Rollalong (Fig. 2), make a hook out of a paper clip. Slide the hook through the cotton reel and place an elastic band over it. Put the long lever through the band and pull the hook through the cotton

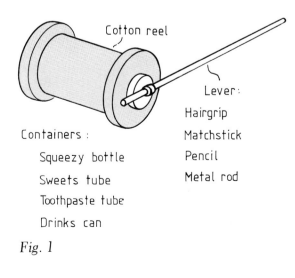

Cotton reel

Lever:
Hairgrip
Matchstick
Pencil
Metal rod

Containers :
Squeezy bottle
Sweets tube
Toothpaste tube
Drinks can

Fig. 1

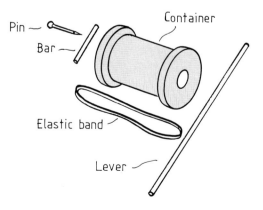

Pin
Bar
Container
Elastic band
Lever

Fig. 2

reel, trapping the lever. When the end of the hook comes out at the end of the cotton reel, slide the small rod through the band. Remove the hook so that the small rod is pulled against the end of the cotton reel. Place some tape over the small rod to stop it slipping when the elastic band is wound up.

Brief 4.1

Choose a bearing for your Rollalong.

Various washers to try :

Steel	Plastic	Paper
Wax	Wood	Glasspaper
Emery cloth	Fabrics	

Fig. 4

choice of material for this washer may help your Rollalong move more quickly along the ground or it may reduce it to a very slow movement. (See Figure 4.)

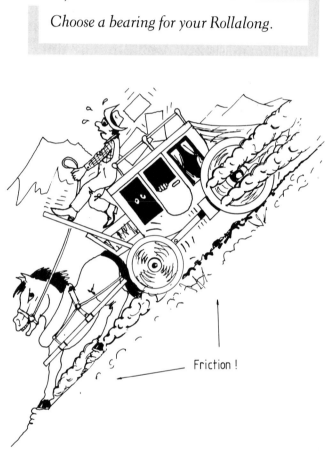

Friction !

Fig. 3

On the stagecoach shown in Figure 3, two types of friction occur. The application of the brakes creates 'useful friction' which is the shoe rubbing against the rim (high friction) and the stagecoach slows down. However, we want the wheels to rotate easily, and here friction must be kept as low as possible. This is called 'non-useful' friction.

With your Rollalong we must reduce the friction that takes place between the lever and the body, by fitting a washer (a bearing). The

Things to do and to find out

1 Find an easy way of threading the elastic band through the hole in the Rollalong.

2 Which washer material gives the worst performance?

3 Which washer material causes the least friction?

4 Which washer would you use for the elastic band to release its energy slowly (control)?

5 Can you find a better low-friction material for the washer?

6 Where, in or around the house, will you find low-friction surfaces?

7 Where on a motor car do you want a lot of (high) friction and where do you want very little (low) friction?

Brief 4.2

Increase the grip of your Rollalong.

Fig. 5

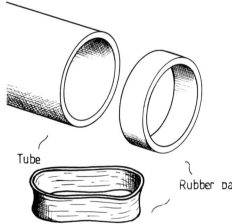

Tube

Rubber band/strips

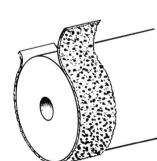

Glasspaper or emery
cloth glued on

Fig. 6

Motor cars often get stuck in the snow because their tyres are too smooth. Tractors have no problems because their tyres give a better grip (Fig. 5). You may find your Rollalong suffers from the same problem as the car.

Figure 6 shows some ways of solving this problem. Can you think of any others? Remember – the rougher the surfaces, the higher the friction and the better the grip!

Things to do and to find out

1 What is the steepest hill your Rollalong can climb using one of the methods shown?

2 How will you measure the slope (gradient)?

3 Make a vehicle to travel over uneven ground.

4 What is the best surface for your vehicle to travel along quickly?

5 Why does the Rollalong tend to lift on the side where the lever touches the ground?

6 Make the largest Rollalong you can from materials you find in the home.

Brief 4.3

Design and build a two-levered motor (Photo 2).

Photo 2

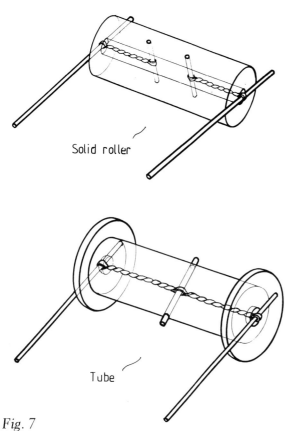

Solid roller

Tube

Fig. 7

One of the problems of the Rollalong you have built is that it tends not to go in a straight line. This is because the lever acts on one end of the body and *torque* tries to raise the other end. Adding another lever to the other end of the body may overcome this twisting effect (torque). Figure 7 shows two ways of doing this.

Things to do and to find out

1 Explain the difference in the performance of your Rollalong when you use two levers.

2 What happens when you use (a) long and (b) short levers?

3 Which makes the Rollalong go faster – short fat rubber bands or long thin ones?

4 Does the number of bands in your 'motor' make any difference?

5 Reduce the friction between the lever ends and the ground by adding wheels. What effect does this have?

6 Does having the levers in front of the Rollalong make it work better or worse?

Brief 4.4

Design your own rubber-powered vehicle (Photo 3).

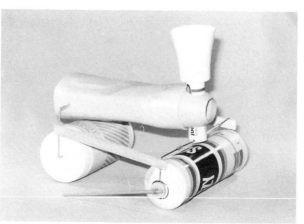

Photo 3

You should now be able to change your rubber band motor to make your Rollalong go faster or slower. Design a vehicle to carry as large a load as possible or to travel as fast as possible. First decide on its maximum dimensions and length and thickness of the rubber bands to be used.

Things to do and to find out

1 What is the largest load your vehicle will carry over one metre?

2 What is the time taken for your vehicle to travel five metres?

3 Now join two or more motor units together to improve your vehicle's performance.

4 From what materials can the body be made?

5 How are the motors to be joined?

6 Draw a graph to compare the number of turns on the rubber band and the distance travelled (see Brief 8.2).

LAMPS

Introduction

If we link a battery and a bulb (Fig. 1), the bulb will light. We call this a *circuit* because electricity from the battery can flow through the wire to the bulb and back again (in the same way that water flows along a hose pipe when a tap is turned on). Figure 2 shows how to draw this circuit using symbols.

Fig. 1

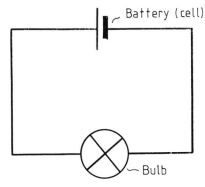

Fig. 2

If we make a break in the wires, the bulb will go out (Fig. 3). This is because we have introduced a switch into our basic circuit.

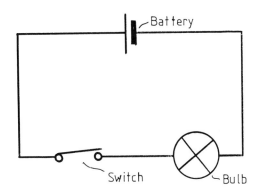

Fig. 3

NOTE

Make sure your battery and bulb are of the same *voltage*. The voltage is shown on the side of the battery and on the side of the bulb. A single-cell battery gives 1.5 volts. Other types of batteries can give 3 volts, 4.5 volts or 6 volts.

Brief 5.1

Design and make a simple electric lamp (Photo 1).

Photo 1

Miner's helmet

Street lamp

Fig. 4

In Figure 4 a light is being used to shine in areas that are dark. Using our simple circuit, it is possible to make a useful lamp.

SAFETY NOTE

Do not use mains voltage (240 volts). Use only 1.5–6 volt batteries.

At one end of a suitable strip of wood attach the lamp holder by making a small lamp bracket that slides into the slot of the holder (Fig. 5). Glue or screw it to the end of the wood. At the other end make a switch as in Figure 6 and fix it to this wooden handle.

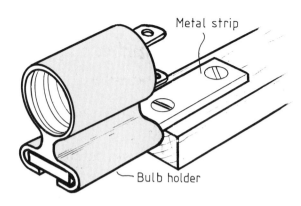

Metal strip

Bulb holder

Fig. 5

In the middle, position the battery (Fig. 7) and, using cable (wire), complete the circuit. Remove about 15 mm of the plastic covering (insulation) from the ends of the wire and twist the strands together. Wrap the bared ends around the pins and push the pins hard into the handle, trapping the wire.

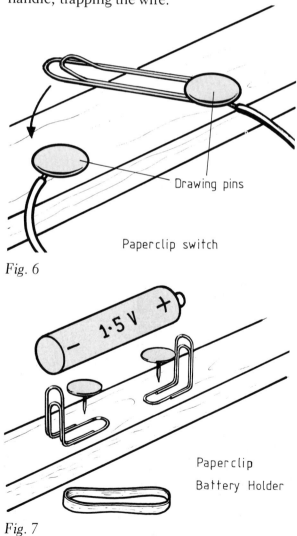

Drawing pins

Paperclip switch

Fig. 6

1·5 V

Paperclip Battery Holder

Fig. 7

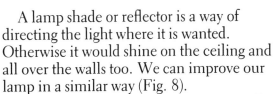

Things to do and to find out

1 Why do you need to twist the ends of the wire strands together?

2 How will you fix the wires to the bulb holder?

3 Can you improve the method of holding the battery in place?

4 Work out the lengths of the wire you need.

5 Can you make a better switch?

6 How will you keep the cable neatly in place?

7 Can you improve on the way in which the wire is fixed to the pins?

Brief 5.2

Design a lamp to shine a light in one direction only (Photo 2).

Photo 2

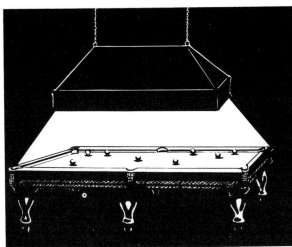

Fig. 8 Lamp over a snooker table

A lamp shade or reflector is a way of directing the light where it is wanted. Otherwise it would shine on the ceiling and all over the walls too. We can improve our lamp in a similar way (Fig. 8).

In Figure 9 a yogurt pot around the bulb directs the light towards the front. We can direct the light to the sides using a piece of aluminium as in Figure 10, or we can make it focus on a small area by fixing the bulb into a plastic toothpaste tube (Fig. 11).

Yogurt carton

Fig. 9

Polished metal curved reflector - cut from drinks can

Fig. 10

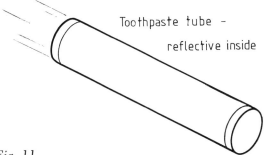

Toothpaste tube - reflective inside

Fig. 11

Things to do and to find out

1 How is your shade going to be fixed on?

2 Why is aluminium a good material to use for a reflector?

3 How can you make your yogurt pot a better reflector?

4 What is the best-shaped reflector to give a straight (parallel) beam of light?

5 How can you make your reflector adjustable?

Brief 5.3

Design a mini-lamp (Photo 3).

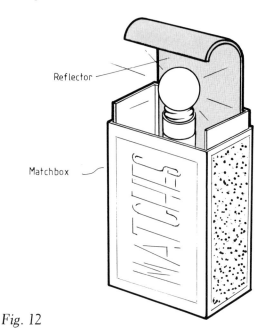

Photo 3

Figure 12 shows one idea.

Reflector

Matchbox

Fig. 12

Mini-lamps can be made from many existing packages, e.g. large matchboxes, sweet tubes etc., or you can build your own. Remember to allow for the shape and size of battery you are to use.

Things to do and to find out

1 What is the best-shaped container to fit your battery?

2 Where is the best place to fit the bulb?

3 What is the best-shaped reflector for your design?

4 How can the battery be held in place?

5 How will the lamp be opened to allow the battery to be changed?

6 Attach your lamp to the wall. Use clips, magnets etc.

Brief 5.4

Design a flexible lamp (Photo 4).

Photo 4

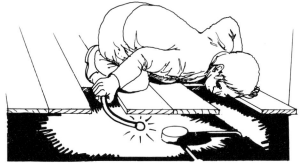

Fig. 13 There may be difficulty in seeing!

Quite often we need to shine a light in an awkward place (Fig. 13). A mini-lamp will be no use. A lamp that can be adjusted to get into these awkward places may be necessary.

You may be able to make a lamp using a soft plastic tube and pushing a solid rod (a stiff piece of wire) through the centre (Fig. 14). When you bend the tube you actually bend the rod and it stays that way until you alter it.

Or you could make a lamp with the stem in three pieces or more that are held together with screws, so that you can change the position of the lamp (Fig. 15).

Things to do and to find out

1 How can you attach the battery, switch and bulb holder to the body?
2 What materials can you use for the body?
3 What must you do to make sure the lamp does not fall over?
4 How will you make the moving (swivel) joint?
5 What is the longest reach of your lamp?

Brief 5.5

Design a switch for your lamp.

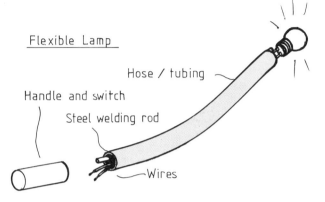

Flexible Lamp

Hose / tubing

Handle and switch

Steel welding rod

Wires

Fig. 14 A *flexible lamp*

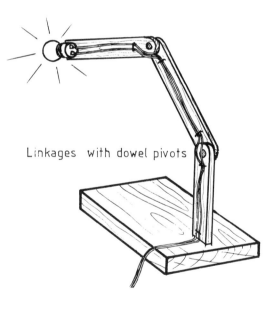

Linkages with dowel pivots

OR Dowel and rod joints

Fig. 15

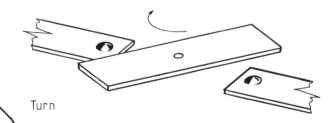

Press

Pull

Turn

Fig. 16 *Switches*

There are many different types of switches, e.g. push, pull, turn, toggle etc. (Fig. 16).

You may decide that when you pick up the lamp it should automatically switch on. Perhaps you want your lamp to come on when you put it down. If you wall-mount your lamp, you may be able to design a switch that operates when you turn the lamp. Work out how you can do this for your lamp.

Brief 5.6

Design a method to adjust the brightness of a lamp source.

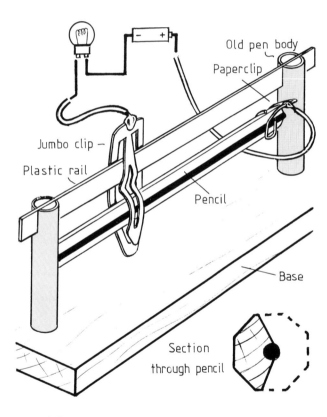

Old pen body

Paperclip

Jumbo clip

Plastic rail

Pencil

Base

Section through pencil

Fig. 17

In many rooms today the brightness of the lights can be adjusted (controlled) by a switch on the wall (a 'dimmer' switch). It is possible to adjust the amount of light given out by your lamp and, later on, you will find this is useful in other projects too (Fig. 17).

The pencil 'lead' (actually graphite) acts as a resistor to the flow of the electrical current. A paper clip is fixed to the pencil near one end and a hair grip is fixed so that it slides along the rail away from the paper-clip connection – the further away, the greater the resistance and therefore any bulb in the circuit will begin to go dim. Whilst they are close together, the lamp or bulb will be bright. This is called a *rheostat*.

Things to do and to find out

1 Design a way of improving the contact.
2 What length of pencil is required?
3 How will you fix the pencil to the pen tops?
4 Where else could this idea be useful?
5 With what voltage battery and bulb is this successful?
6 How will you fix the wires to the grips?

Brief 5.7

Design a Battleship game (Photo 5).

Photo 5

You have probably played Battleships using pencil and paper. Now you can design a game using the simple circuit knowledge you have acquired.

Obtain a piece of plywood about 100 mm square and draw the lines as in Figure 18. Lightly hammer panel pins through the board so that they protrude from the other side.

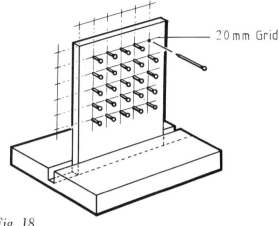

— 20 mm Grid

Fig. 18

Decide upon the type and number of ships to be used, e.g. a submarine covers two pins, a cruiser three pins etc. Wrap wire around these pins (Fig. 19) using a pair of pliers to help you. Change (modify) your simple circuit to allow you to use the ends of wires in place of your switch (Fig. 20). You are now ready to let a friend find (trace) the joined-up pins.

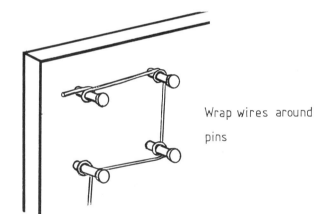

Wrap wires around pins

Fig. 19

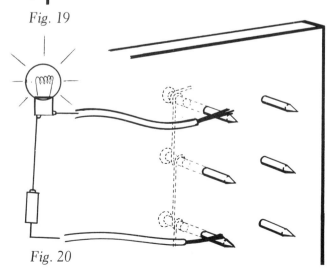

Fig. 20

Things to do and to find out

1 The board you have made needs supporting to make it free-standing. Sketch three other ways of doing this.

2 Improve the method of touching the pins for better contact (Fig. 21).

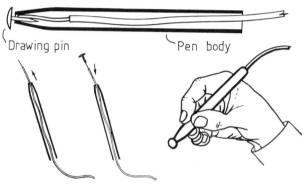

Drawing pin   Pen body

Fig. 21 A contact probe

3 Make a larger board with more pins in it.

4 Make a board to let two people use it at the same time.

5 Using a long piece of wire, thread a continuous circuit of your choice around the pins. Now get your friend to trace this circuit.

6 What other materials could be used for the board?

7 Fit the bulb, bulb holder and battery to the board using ways that have been used in earlier briefs.

STRUCTURES

Introduction

No doubt you have played 'piggyback', where you have tried to push or pull another pair over or tried to turn them around. Eventually you can no longer support your friend or you collapse from the pushing or pulling because you get weaker. In a similar way structures have to withstand pushing (compression), pulling (tension) and turning or twisting forces. If the structures are not strong enough, they will collapse. Structures such as bridges, radio masts, buildings, chairs and skeletons are designed either by people or nature to resist these forces.

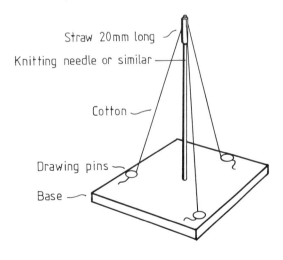

Straw 20mm long

Knitting needle or similar

Cotton

Drawing pins

Base

Fig. 1

Let us look at two of these forces that act on our structure which we will call a Buildamast.

How to make your Buildamast (Fig. 1)

Use similar materials to those suggested.

1 Wrap tape around one end of the rod, until it is a 'push' fit into the straw.

2 Slit the straw in three places at one end, to a depth of 5 mm (Fig. 2).

3 Cut three pieces of cotton approximately one and a half times the rod length and tie a knot on one end of each piece.

4 Thread the knotted end into each slit that you have made in the straw.

5 Fix three drawing pins into the board to form a triangular shape – as far away from the rod as possible.

6 Place the rod in the middle of the board.

7 Take one of the cotton ends and wrap it around a drawing pin. Repeat this for the other two pins.

8 Adjust the cotton to support the rod and press the pins in firmly.

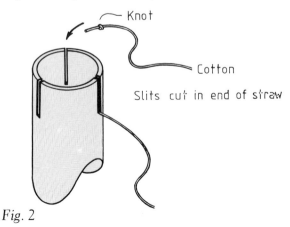

Knot

Cotton

Slits cut in end of straw

Fig. 2

The rod (strut) should now be supported upright by the cotton and pins. Just as in the large radio mast (Photo 1), the forces on the rod are downward through its own weight and are called *compressive* forces. The cotton has been pulled tight, which means that the forces acting through each piece are *tensile*.

Photo 1

Things to do and to find out

1 Gently push down on the straw (simulating the mast's collapse). What has happened to the cotton ties? You will find they are no longer in tension and the mast is tilting.

2 Re-tension the cotton ties by pulling on the cotton ends or by sliding the straw back up the rod.

3 Using scissors, cut one of the ties. The forces holding the rod in place have broken down and the rod collapses. The cutting of the cotton simulates the *shearing* (wire breaking) of the tie.

Build a bridge: Stage 1

Construct a 'starter pack' (Photo 2).
Now that you have completed a Buildamast, let us look at building a structure which

includes *ties* and *struts*. Here is how to construct a bridge using card, paper clips, sticky tape, cotton and buttons – not forgetting a small model car to test your work!

Photo 2

How to make your starter pack
(Figs 3–5)

1 Obtain a piece of plywood 640 mm × 75 mm × 4 mm for a base.

2 Using two candy-stick cartons as pillars, Sellotape the inside piece into position on the base, keeping them 250 mm apart (Fig. 3).

3 Cut a piece of card 400 mm × 55 mm to be a road (Fig. 4).

4 Cut two pieces of card (to slide into carton) and Sellotape them to the underside of the road – 250 mm apart.

5 Assemble the road to the pillars (Fig. 5).

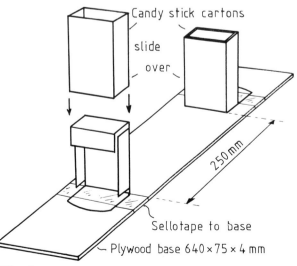

Fig. 3

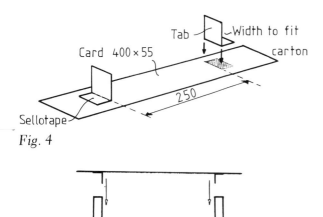

Fig. 4

Fig. 5 *Turn the structure over and slide it into the cartons (as in Fig. 8)*

Things to do and to find out

Place the model car on the road and pull it across the bridge with a piece of cotton tied to your toy. The road 'sags' in the middle and the pillars collapse inwards. Try to explain why this happens. Think of a way to stop this occurring. One answer is shown in the next stage.

Build a bridge: Stage 2

Improve the strength of the bridge by using ties (Photo 3).

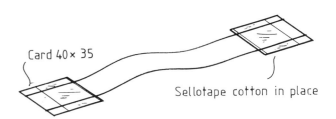

Photo 3

As you follow the bridge design, you will be able to strip it down (dismantle) and re-build it (reassemble) as you progress. This saves time in not having to make numerous bridges.

How to make your tie-strengthened bridge (Figs 6–8)

1 Cut four pieces of card (the inside width of the carton) approximately 40 mm × 35 mm (Fig. 6).

2 Wrap two pieces of cotton around one of the cards and Sellotape them in place.

3 Repeat this on the other end, allowing for a distance of 125 mm of cotton between the cards.

4 Complete steps 2 and 3 of the above for the other two cards.

5 Slide the card into the carton (Fig. 7).

6 Attach the other end to the base, making sure the cotton ties are tight (Fig. 8).

7 Refit the road.

Fig. 6

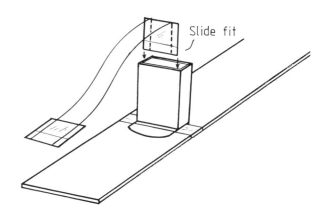

Fig. 7

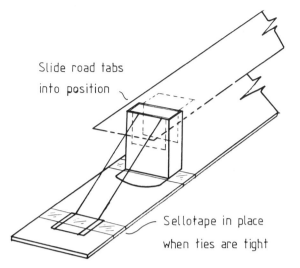

Slide road tabs into position

Sellotape in place when ties are tight

Fig. 8

Things to do and to find out

1 Pull the toy across the bridge. The pillars remain upright and the bridge bends in the middle – but not as much as the starter pack!

2 The cotton is holding the bridge in place and therefore it is acting as ties. Try cutting the cotton on one end of the bridge and see what happens.

3 Make the road stronger to prevent further bending. Move onto stage 3 for one way of solving this problem.

Build a bridge: Stage 3

Improve the strength of the bridge using struts.
    Another way to strengthen your bridge could be to use struts. You may eventually want to build a bridge using struts only or a mixture (combination) of ties and struts (Photo 4).

Photo 4

How to strengthen a bridge using struts (Figs 9–11)

1 Return to your starter pack stage.

2 Cut four straws of length 125 mm.

3 Thread cotton through the straws, to allow them to be set at a width of 55 mm apart (Fig. 9).

4 Sellotape two pieces of card 30 mm × 40 mm into place underneath the road, leaving one end not taped to allow cotton to slide between them (Fig. 10).

5 Fix one end of the pair of straws into position under the road and hold them in place by card and tape.

6 Ensure the other ends jam against the base of the pillar (Fig. 11).

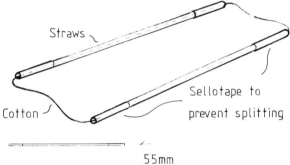

Straws

Cotton

Sellotape to prevent splitting

55mm

Fig. 9

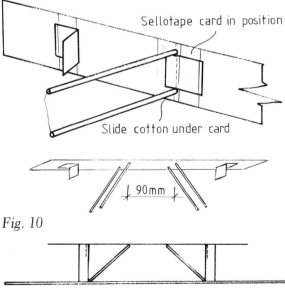

Sellotape card in position

Slide cotton under card

90mm

Fig. 10

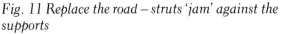

Fig. 11 Replace the road – struts 'jam' against the supports

Things to do and to find out

1 Pull the car across the road: this time the road does not bend in the middle.

2 The struts are holding the bridge in place and are in compression. Try cutting one set of straws and see what happens!

Proceed to the next stage.

Build a bridge: Stage 4

Strengthen the bridge to support greater loads (Photo 5).

Until now the weight (load) of your car has bent the road spanning the pillars. Using these methods of support, the load will have to be increased to cause the road to buckle or distort. (Proving that your bridge is getting stronger.) Add weights to your car to simulate extra load. Bridges have to support hundreds of cars, lorries and buses at once, as well as coping with winds and rain!

Photo 5

How to improve the load-carrying capacity of your bridge (Figs 12–15)

1 Cut a piece of card 400 mm × 90 mm, mark out two rails of 15 mm width and fold (Fig. 12).

2 Remove the previous road and place this card across the pillars (folds down).

3 Pull the car across and you will find the road will support it.

Now progressively increase the load and you find the sides buckle in the middle. Can you explain why this has happened?

4 One way to prevent this buckling is to fix a cotton tie across the weak point (Fig. 13).

5 Repeat the previous test and you will see the bridge has been made much stronger.

6 Reverse the road and repeat the test – does the cotton tie still work as well?

7 The bridge can be made still stronger by reinforcing (strengthening) the sides. Try the ideas in Figures 14 and 15 and retest its load-carrying capabilities.

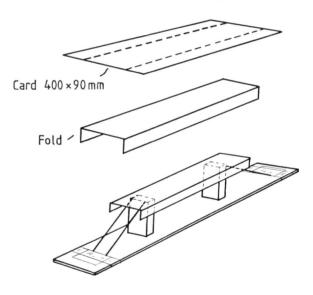

Card 400 × 90 mm

Fold

Fig. 12

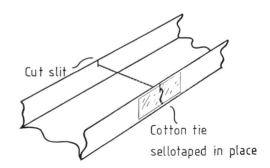

Cut slit

Cotton tie
sellotaped in place

Fig. 13

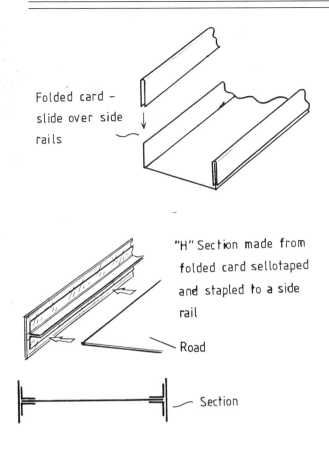

Folded card – slide over side rails ↓

"H" Section made from folded card sellotaped and stapled to a side rail

Road

Section

Fig. 15

How to make your suspension bridge (Fig. 16)

1 Make a road as in stages 1 and 2.

2 Cut slits in the road (Fig. 16).

3 Make two towers from card (Fig. 17).

4 Make tops for towers (Fig. 18).

5 Make four ties with cotton and buttons (Fig. 19).

6 Assemble tower to road and attach base card for the ties (Fig. 20).

7 Assemble ties from the tower to base and from the tower to the road (Fig. 21).

8 Fit tops to the towers.

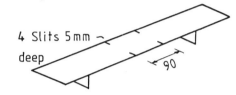

4 Slits 5mm deep   90

Fig. 16

Build a bridge: Stage 5

Build a suspension bridge (Photo 6).

You will have realised by now that the starter pack is using the candy stick cartons as pillars or in fact as struts – because they support compressive loads (weights). Another way to build a bridge project is to make a suspension bridge. This bridge supports loads by using ties which are in tension.

Photo 6

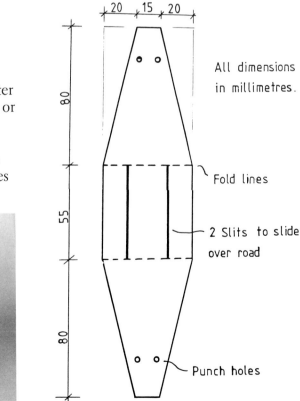

20 15 20

All dimensions in millimetres.

80

Fold lines

55

2 Slits to slide over road

80

Punch holes

Fig. 17

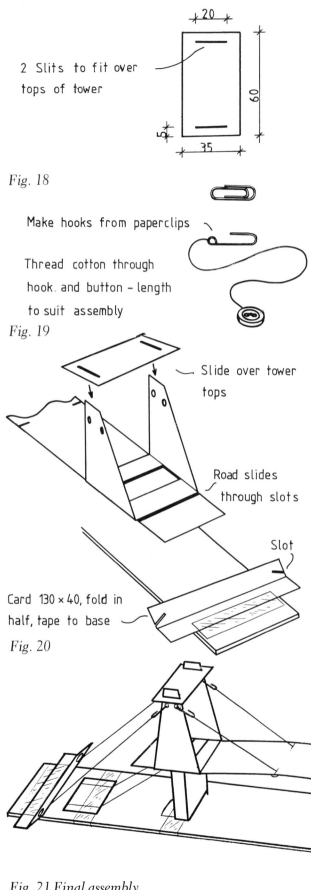

2 Slits to fit over
tops of tower

Fig. 18

Make hooks from paperclips

Thread cotton through
hook. and button – length
to suit assembly

Fig. 19

Slide over tower
tops

Road slides
through slots

Slot

Card 130 × 40, fold in
half, tape to base

Fig. 20

Fig. 21 Final assembly

Pull your car across the road and increase the weight to test the strength of the bridge.

You should now understand a little more about structures. The 'build a bridge' project using card is an easy and quick way of looking at principles. The ways shown of fitting parts together are as a guide only. If you think you can improve on them – do so! Go to the library to find out more about suspension bridges: the Humber Bridge etc.

Brief 6.1: Tower

Design a tower to be as tall as possible and to be built of cans or straws.

The introduction to Buildamast shows a radio mast being supported by guide wires (ties). If these were not used, the mast would very quickly fall over.

Things to do and to find out

1 How many cans can you stack before they become unstable (fall over)?

2 Fit ties to your tower.

3 Do lighter materials appear to be better to use than heavy ones? (Fill the cans and find out.)

4 Try blowing your tower over with wind (use a vacuum cleaner or a hair dryer).

5 How many ties do you need to support your tower well?

6 Place a weight on the top of your tower. What is the effect on its balance?

7 Try glueing or taping your cans together.

8 Push the tower at the top and then at the bottom. Explain any differences you notice.

9 List ways of fixing ties to the cans and the floor.

10 Include a light on top of your tower – use the basic circuit from section 5 on lamps.

11 How can you fit the straws firmly together? Sketch your ideas.

Brief 6.2: Stilts

Design a structure to make yourself taller.

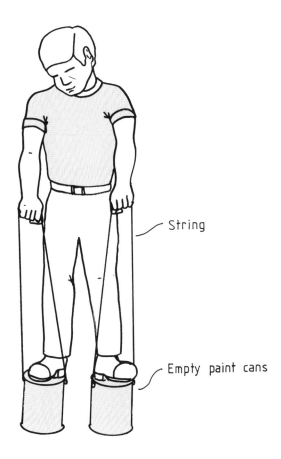

Fig. 22 Stilts

When you visit the circus there are many examples of struts and ties. The Big Top is supported by very large poles (struts). Bracing wires (ties) hold the struts and the tent canvas firmly in position. Clowns use stilts (struts) to make themselves very tall. The tightrope walker balances on a tie stretched between two struts!

Can you make a simple pair of mini-stilts? One way of doing this is using large tins and string as shown in Figure 22.

Things to do and to find out

1 What materials are strong enough to support your weight and how can you test them?

2 Which parts in Figure 22 are taking the compressive (pushing) forces and which are taking the tensile (pulling) forces? Label them as struts and ties.

3 How will you fix them together?

4 Can the structure be made from some form of tube (toilet roll, Smartie packets, spray cans etc.)?

5 Sketch the many different examples of ties and struts that you might see in a circus.

6 Make a pair of mini-stilts that can be strapped to your legs.

7 What length will the ties have to be for comfort? Measure yourself and find out.

Brief 6.3: Car ramp

Design a 'car-jump' ramp.

Motor-cycle and motor-car stunt riders use a sloping ramp to help them clear a number of vehicles. Using the information previously given, design a structure to demonstrate this technique with model cars.

Things to do and to find out

1 What shape will the ramp have to be?

2 How strong will the ramp have to be?

3 What materials can be used for the structure?

4 Do larger, heavier cars 'jump' further?

5 What effect will altering the slope have on results?

6 Sketch your ideas and label the struts and ties.

7 Can you make your ramp adjustable?

8 When you have built your structure, mark out where to position your model for jumps using (a) one car, (b) two cars, (c) three cars etc.

Brief 6.4: Roof

Design a structure to span the largest area possible without posts or pillars in the way.

Many sports complexes and exhibition centres require the maximum area possible to mount exhibitions or to carry out sports competitions. Pillars can reduce this area and block people's views.

When you are designing this model structure, you must make it strong enough to support the weight of a housebrick when it is placed on the centre of the roof. Only straws, cotton, card, pins and Sellotape are to be used.

Things to do and to find out

1 What is the weight of a housebrick?

2 How strong is cotton (if used)? Explain how you can find this out.

3 Try using only four corner pillars when designing the structure.

4 What is the largest area possible that can be covered using your method of construction?

5 Explain how you strengthened your structure.

6 Sketch your design and label the struts and ties.

7 Find out and describe the design of one such structure in your area.

Brief 6.5: Bridge

Design a cantilever bridge that will support a vehicle carrying a carton of milk across it. The distance between the towers is to be at least 300 mm and the material used is to be card.

Many bridges have to be raised to allow ships to pass under them. You will need to design into your structure a means of raising and lowering the bridge.

Things to do and to find out

1 What type of structure will your cantilever bridge need to be?

2 How will it be strengthened?

3 Are you able to use ties and struts?

4 From what materials will these be made?

5 What type of mechanism can be used?

6 How many ways can you think of to raise or lower the bridge?

7 Research bridges in your school library.

WINDCATCHER

Introduction

Natural forms of energy are very important to us as we begin to use up our supplies of oil, coal and gas. Wind is a natural form of energy, and for a very long time people have used this energy to drive windmills. These in turn have been used to drive generators or crush corn.

You can design and make a similar device which we will call a Windcatcher (Photo 1).

Photo 1

Fig. 1 A Windcatcher

How to make your Windcatcher
(Figures 1 and 2)

1 Select a plastic container as a basic structure.

2 Drill two holes opposite each other near the top of your container to give a bearing (running fit) (Fig. 2a).

3 Make a crank from material such as a coathanger. This piece of rod has to be long enough to have two bends made in it and still be far enough away from the bottle to let the blades turn and not hit the bottle (Fig. 2b).

4 Fit the crank into the bottle by wriggling it through one hole and out of the other. The plastic is flexible (bends easily) and allows you to do this (Fig. 2c).

5 Cut two pieces of dowelling, drill a hole in one end and saw a slot in the other (Fig. 2d).

6 Make two blades which, when assembled, will fit into the slot in the dowel and will rotate without coming below the base of the bottle or hitting the sides (Fig. 2e).

7 Pin the blades to the dowel to keep them in place (Fig. 2f).

8 Make two clips to stop the bent arm sliding sideways (Fig. 2g).

9 A means of fitting the bottle to a post in the garden is necessary. Sketch at least two ideas on paper.

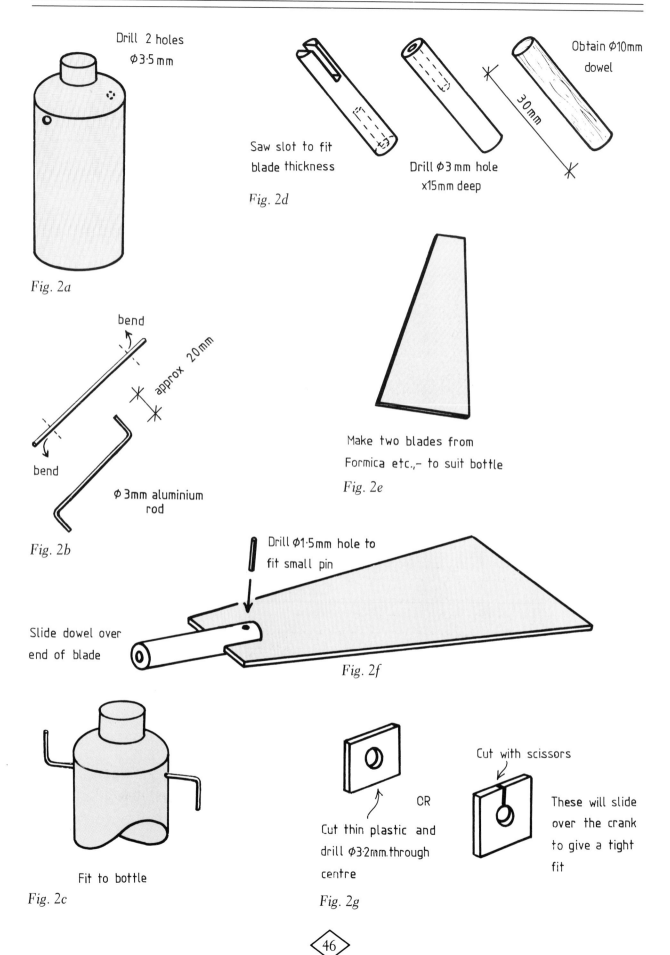

Drill 2 holes
⌀3·5mm

Fig. 2a

Saw slot to fit
blade thickness

Fig. 2d

Drill ⌀3mm hole
x15mm deep

Obtain ⌀10mm
dowel

30mm

bend

approx 20mm

bend

⌀3mm aluminium
rod

Fig. 2b

Make two blades from
Formica etc.,– to suit bottle

Fig. 2e

Drill ⌀1·5mm hole to
fit small pin

Slide dowel over
end of blade

Fig. 2f

Fit to bottle

Fig. 2c

Cut thin plastic and
drill ⌀3·2mm. through
centre

OR

Fig. 2g

Cut with scissors

These will slide
over the crank
to give a tight
fit

NOTE

To make your Windcatcher more interesting, colour a face or design on paper and place it inside the bottle.

Brief 7.1

Find out how to make your Windcatcher work well (efficiently) (Photo 2).

Photo 2

The Windcatcher works in a way that is different from a windmill. The blades will turn if the wind hits it as in Figure 3 or Figure 4. The fin used on garden devices is not necessary on yours.

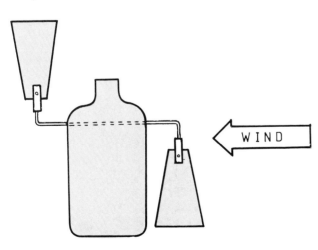

Fig. 3

Fig. 4

Some shapes to try!

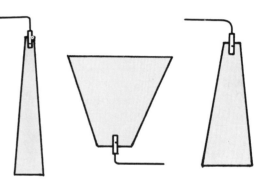

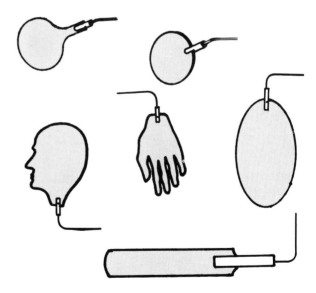

Fig. 5

By trying different-shaped blades there are many interesting points to be investigated (Fig. 5).

Things to do and to find out

Use the 'normal' blade, as in the introduction.

1 Push the blades onto the ends of the arms, and place the bottle in front of a vacuum cleaner with the tube connected to the 'blowing' end, or use a hair dryer.

2 Adjust the blade angles so that the arms rotate (Fig. 6).

3 Adjust the blades to obtain (a) a fast and (b) a slow speed of rotation.

4 Adjust the blades to change the *direction* of rotation.

5 Explain the results of steps 2–4.

6 Make some blades similar to those in Figure 5 and place them in order of efficiency (best to worst).

7 Blades may be shaped or coloured to make the Windcatcher more attractive to look at. Sketch some other ideas.

8 Design a pattern/face on paper and fit it inside the container.

9 You have blown air in one direction at the bottle; turn it through 90° and direct air at it now (Figs 3 and 4).

10 Repeat the previous experiments and explain what happens.

Your Windcatcher will function (work) better as shown in Figure 3 and will be difficult to rotate as shown in Figure 4. This is because of the leverage effect and forces opposing each other. Explain this in greater detail.

Brief 7.2

Improve the design of your Windcatcher by using pulleys to make a moving vehicle (Photo 3).

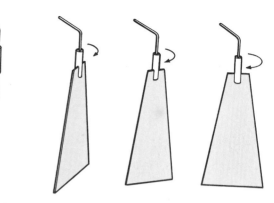

Fig. 6

Photo 3

You have used wind energy to power your Windcatcher and set the blades to a 'best angle'. Use this knowledge to change this energy into useful work and move a vehicle!

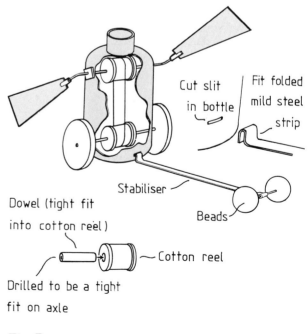

Cut slit in bottle

Fit folded mild steel strip

Stabiliser

Dowel (tight fit into cotton reel)

Beads

Cotton reel

Drilled to be a tight fit on axle

Fig. 7

Take your Windcatcher from brief 7.1 and add two wheels to the bottom (Fig. 7). Include a body so that you have a four-wheeled device. (Section 3 on the Movealong may help here.)

Things to do and to find out

1 Use one pulley to transfer the energy.

2 Figure 8 shows two pulleys using cotton reels – try this idea.

3 The pulleys on the bent arms will have to be assembled *before* you bend the arms:
   (a) How will you do this and keep them in the correct position?
   (b) How will you bend the arms when they are assembled through the bottle? (It *is* possible.)

4 How big should each pulley be?

5 You may need an interference (tight fit) or a running (bearing) fit between the pulleys, wheels and axles. How will you achieve this?

6 Where is friction present and how can it be reduced?

7 What other ways are there to make pulleys? Sketch some ideas and make them.

8 How will the side rail (structure) be fitted to the bottle?

9 In Figure 7, the rear wheels must be free to rotate. How can this be done?

10 The side rails will not stop the bottle from tilting – further support using ties or struts will be necessary to keep it upright. (See section 6, Build a bridge, for help.)

11 Test your Windcatcher over different types of surface and suggest the best one. Explain your reasons.

NOTE

The elastic around the pulley to the rear wheel is used in sewing and is called 'shirring elastic'.

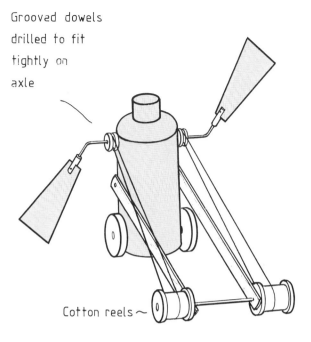

Grooved dowels drilled to fit tightly on axle

Cotton reels

Fig. 8

Brief 7.3

Propel your vehicle using a double-crank method.

The crank is a very useful mechanical device that helps to change one direction of motion to another. You may decide to use a single crank in your design and will find that it tends to 'rock' forwards and backwards only. Make one and compare it with the 'double-crank' method which is guaranteed to work (Fig. 9).

Things to do and to find out

1 How will you make a single crank? (See brief 3.1.)

2 Make linkages to fit between the cranks. The linkages can be made from items such as lollypop sticks, wire, plastic, Meccano/steel strip. One problem you may have is sliding the linkage over the formed crank inside the container!

3 How will you keep the linkage from sliding off the crank?

4 Make a double crank as seen in Figure 9.

5 Explain why the double crank works better.

6 The fit of a shaft is always a very important design consideration. See if you can explain where the following are used.
   (a) Clearance (loose) fit.
   (b) Interference (tight) fit.
   (c) Running (bearing) fit.

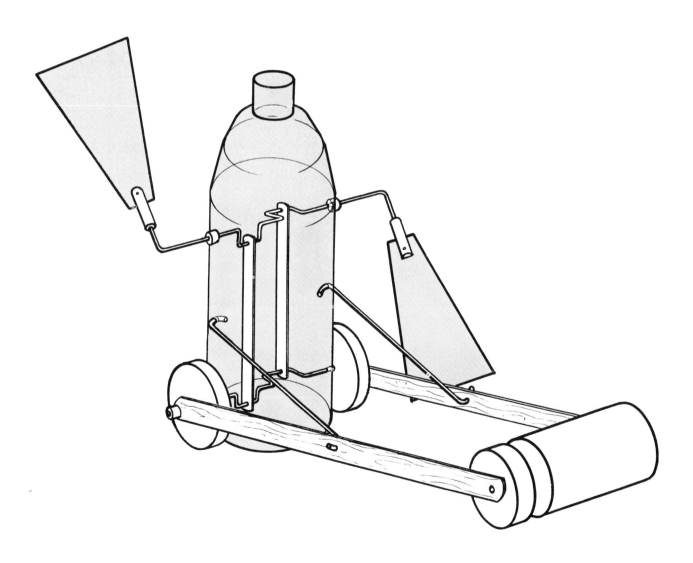

Fig. 9 A double-crank Windcatcher

ELASTIC ENERGY

Introduction

Energy exists in many forms, such as heat, light, sound etc. One form of energy is called 'strain energy'. The simplest form of strain energy is a stretched elastic band or spring (Fig. 1). On release, this strain energy (potential energy) is changed into a movement (kinetic energy) and the stone is catapulted forward.

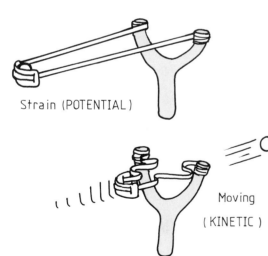

Strain (POTENTIAL)

Moving (KINETIC)

Fig. 1

If we can control this energy, we can use it. One way is to apply it to a vehicle. An example of such a vehicle is shown in Photo 1, this time constructed from Meccano.

Photo 1

Brief 8.1

Design a vehicle that uses an elastic band as its energy source.

Ensure your vehicle has an overall length of 300 mm so that the elastic band can be fully stretched.

By using small wheels on one end and large wheels on the other you will be able to compare their different effects. The elastic band can be attached as shown in Figure 2 so that it releases the energy smoothly each time. The string is looped over a small headed screw. Removing the head and sawing a slot in the end of the stem will assist in testing.

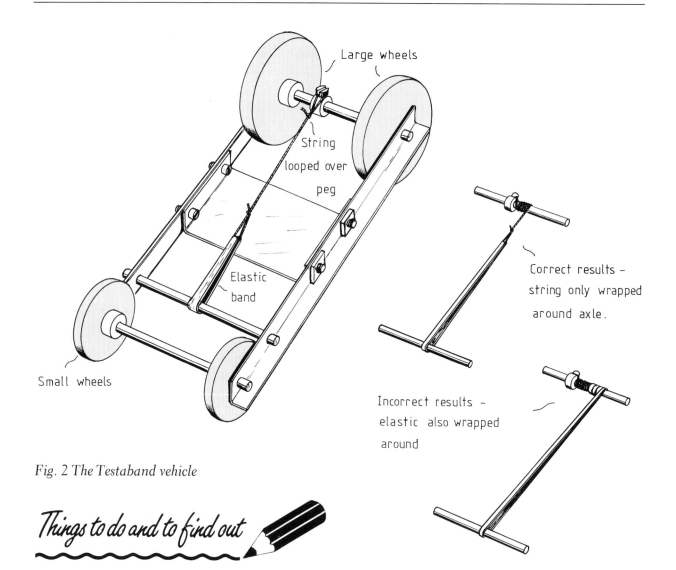

Fig. 2 The Testaband vehicle

Things to do and to find out

1 Hook the loop of the string onto the pin on the rear axle and 'wind up' the rear drive wheels (large size). Place the vehicle on the floor and release it. Measure how far the vehicle travels.

2 Repeat the above using the small wheels as the drive wheels. Measure how far the vehicle travels.

3 Which wheels caused the vehicle to travel further? Why?

4 Which wheels caused the vehicle to accelerate (gain speed) quicker? Why?

5 With the small wheels on the rear axle, wind the string around the axle to stretch the band to its limit. Are you able to make the wheels spin (slip) before they grip and

move forward? How can you prevent wheel slip? Repeat the experiment with the large wheels. Why does it not happen this time?

6 Now explain why the pin for hooking the string onto the rear axle has been offset.

7 What happens to the vehicle if the loop on the string does not release properly? Explain why this is unsatisfactory.

8 Place a weight onto the vehicle and explain how the vehicle's performance is affected.

9 How can you now make the vehicle move the same distance as in step 8 above prior to adding the weight?

10 The vehicle shown has been made from Meccano parts. Make yours from other materials.

11 Why should you not allow the band to stretch around the axle?

12 Try running the vehicle up a slope. Does it still travel as fast or as far as on the flat?

You have now tested your vehicle. But if you want to become a technologist, you have to be able to record and show a vehicle's performance far more accurately. To do this you will need to study in more detail the ways in which an elastic band behaves. Move on to the next brief.

Brief 8.2

Complete a graph to help you 'predict' the distance your vehicle will travel. Use the method shown in Figure 3.

Graphs are really quite easy to complete and will give us a great deal of information. We are going to use two sets of readings only. Remember! the results given in Fig. 4 are examples only, as *no* two elastic bands are the same.

As the string is wound around the rear drive axle to stretch the band, we use this as one set of readings and call it 'turns'. When the vehicle moves across the floor the distance travelled can be measured in any units; feet, metres or even 'tiles' if your floor happens to be evenly tiled. For our second reading we will use 'tiles' as the distance travelled.

Obtaining accurate results is very important and you have to be very careful in how you carry this out. Firstly the 'slack' in the band has to be removed. Wind the string around the axle until there is no slack and note the position of the pin on the axle. From now on, that is where you will start each time you increase the turns on the axle.

With this initial setting you can now turn the rear (drive) axle once. Place the vehicle on the floor in line with a chosen tile and release it.

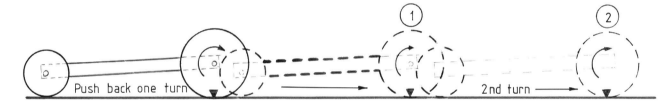

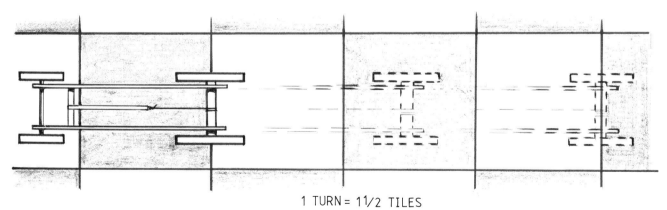

1 TURN = 1 1/2 TILES

Fig. 3 Testing the band

TURNS	1	2	3	4	5	
TILES	1	2½	3¾	6½	9½	

Fig. 4 A data table

The vehicle will move forward perhaps 1½ tiles. Increase the number of turns progressively (in steps of one) and count the units (tiles) travelled each time. As you carry out this test, put the results in the data box as shown in Figure 4, ready to be transferred onto the graph (Fig. 5).

When you complete the graph, note the vertical (upright) axis is in turns and the horizontal in units (distance). Where each pair of readings meet, place a cross. An elastic band is not going to give accurate results every time, and when you have plotted all the points, draw a smooth curve (through) the points. This eliminates (gets rid of) some of the errors that can occur. (Note the 'lump' in the middle of the curve in Figure 5.)

Things to do and to find out

1 Select a point on your graph and 'set' your vehicle with the number of turns shown. See if it does travel the distance you would expect.

2 Repeat this experiment a number of times.

3 How accurate are your results?

4 If your results do not follow the graph, list the problems that could cause them.

5 Test your vehicle against another vehicle for speed and distance. Account for any large differences.

6 Choose a vehicle with small wheel drive and a vehicle with large wheel drive. How would you set the vehicles to travel the same distance?

7 How could you make your vehicle travel (a) further (b) faster?

8 Increase the weight of the vehicle and show results on a graph.

This brief is to help you learn how to complete graphs. Remember – as the elastic band releases its energy, the vehicle moves forward. When all the band energy is gone, the vehicle continues under its own 'steam' (inertia).

Brief 8.3

Complete a graph to show the stretch/strain relationship and energy in an elastic band.

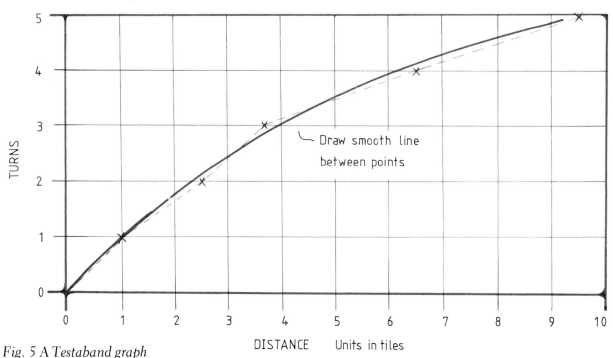

Fig. 5 A *Testaband graph*

In stretching an elastic band (Fig. 6), a pulling or *tensile* force is being applied to it. The elastic band is under tension. When the force is released, the band will return to its original state where no tension is present.

If we can stretch the band a known length and measure the force applied, we can plot the results on a graph. The method used is similar to one of the many tests that are carried out on other materials. However, the equipment used for checking or measuring this pulling (tensile) strength of materials such as steel is expensive and is not usually available in schools. Nevertheless, you can check or measure the tensile strength of an elastic band instead.

Things to do and to find out

Make a data table as in Figure 7, completing the boxes as you take the readings at each stage.

1 Obtain an elastic band and spring balance (you can make one yourself – see Briefs 15.1 and 15.2).

2 Make a hook to attach the elastic band (Fig. 6).

3 Loop one end of the band over the rod.

4 Hook the balance through the other loop and pull to remove any slack in band (ensuring that the balance is reading zero).

5 Set a rule with either the nought against the end of the band with the balance hook in it or as shown in Figure 6.

6 Pull on the balance until 1 newton is shown on the scale, and in the data box record the length the band has stretched (Fig. 7).

7 Repeat this in steps of 1 newton.

8 Observe what happens to the thickness of the band as you pull on it.

9 What other changes in the band occur?

10 Release the tension on the band each time and check to see if it has permanently stretched.

11 Plot the results on your graph (Fig. 8).

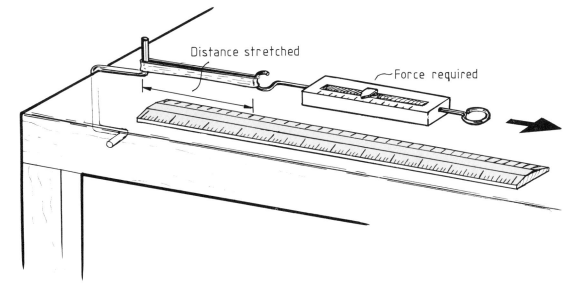

Fig. 6 *Testing the band*

DISTANCE (mm)	15	40	70	90	125	150
FORCE (Newtons)	1	2	3	4	5	6

Fig. 7 *A data table*

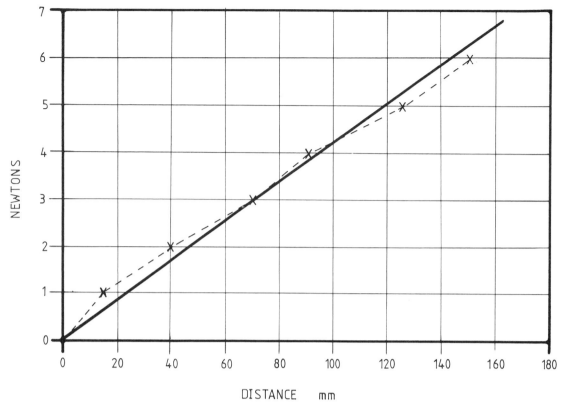

Fig. 8 A Testaband graph

12 Repeat the experiments with the same band – but do not break it. State what changes have taken place.

13 *Now* increase the load until the elastic band breaks.

14 Show on your graph the point at which the elastic band breaks.

15 Try placing two bands together and repeat the test. Plot the results on your first graph. Are the results what you expected? Can you explain any difference between this graph and your graph of a single elastic band in tension?

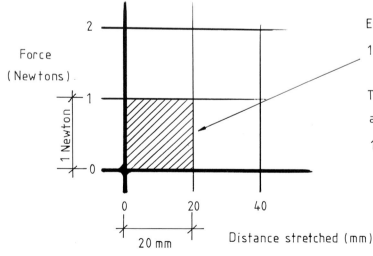

Energy in 1 square =

1 Newton × 20 mm = <u>20 Nmm</u>

Therefore when elastic is stretched a distance of 120 mm, TOTAL ENERGY = 15 squares × 20 Nmm = <u>300 Nmm</u>

Fig. 9

Energy in the band

Each square on the graph measures 1 newton by 20 mm (Fig. 9). The energy for each square is therefore 1 × 20 or 20 newton millimetres (20 Nmm). The area *under* the graph is the energy stored in the band. In Figure 10 the horizontal base line shows the band has been stretched 120 mm. By counting all the squares in this row and all those to its left 'under the graph', you will work out the energy required to stretch the band 120 mm.

Once again, to reduce error, only count the boxes that the graph shows as *larger than a half box* and do not count those less than a half box (Fig. 10). The total 'energy' required to stretch the band by 120 mm is therefore 15 squares or 15 × 20 = 300 Nmm.

Using this procedure look at the graph (Fig. 5) and work out how much energy is required to make the vehicle travel:

1 4 tiles (or units).
2 6 tiles (or units).
3 9 tiles (or units).

Many small toys use wind-up springs to provide the energy to drive them. Springs come in many forms: under tension (Fig. 11), compression (pushing) (Fig. 12), wound-up (Fig. 13). Remove the elastic band from your first vehicle and replace it with a small tension spring.

Brief 8.4: Testaspring

Compare results obtained using a spring-powered vehicle against a rubber-powered vehicle.

Things to do and to find out

1 Draw up another data table and graph as with the elastic band experiment to show the tension in the spring balance.

2 How do the results of the spring graph compare with the single elastic band graph?

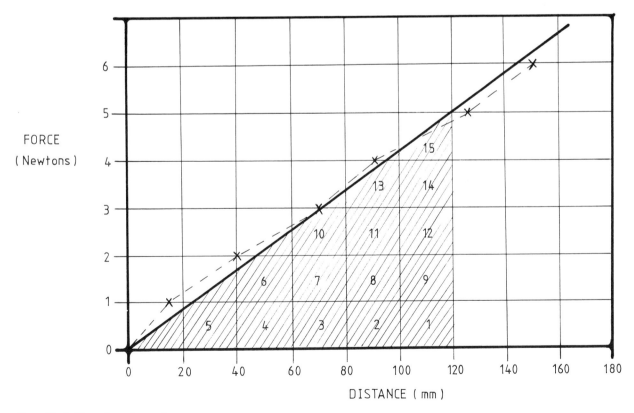

Fig. 10 A Testaband graph

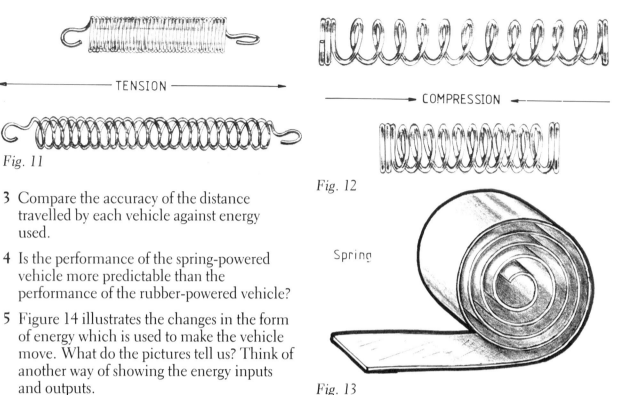

TENSION

Fig. 11

COMPRESSION

Fig. 12

Spring

Fig. 13

3 Compare the accuracy of the distance travelled by each vehicle against energy used.

4 Is the performance of the spring-powered vehicle more predictable than the performance of the rubber-powered vehicle?

5 Figure 14 illustrates the changes in the form of energy which is used to make the vehicle move. What do the pictures tell us? Think of another way of showing the energy inputs and outputs.

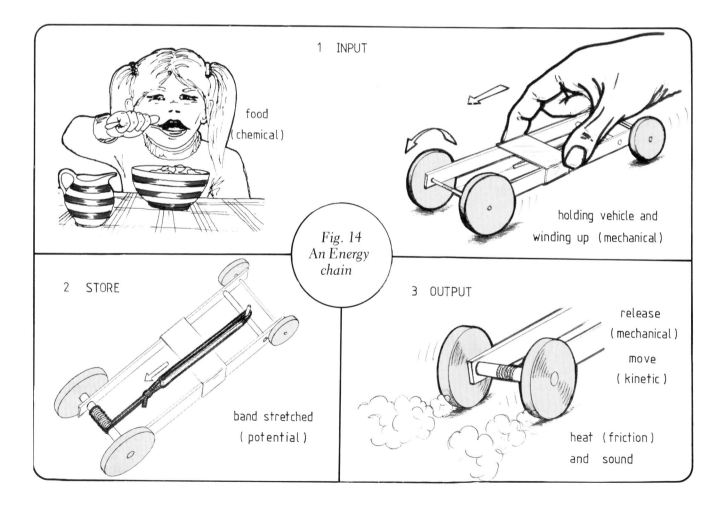

1 INPUT

food (chemical)

holding vehicle and winding up (mechanical)

Fig. 14 An Energy chain

2 STORE

band stretched (potential)

3 OUTPUT

release (mechanical)

move (kinetic)

heat (friction) and sound

BRAINSTORMER

Introduction

Brainstorming is where a group of people get together and try to find a solution to a problem by generating and pooling ideas. Quite often one person cannot be very inventive by himself or herself, but once other people start to suggest solutions this begins to 'trigger' other ideas. The result is a large number of ideas from which the best solution can be chosen.

Brainstorming is a method used by designers throughout industry and commerce. Most designing is not original, but is an improvement or slight alteration of something already in existence.

We are going to look at a basic unit (Fig. 1 and Photo 1). See in how many different ways this unit can be used. Remember: as we work through the Brainstormer *you* may be able to improve or think of other ways in which the unit could be adapted and suggest better materials for it.

Photo 1

This particular project is designed so that you will learn about *levers*, *fulcrum*, *load* and *effort*, but don't let these terms put you off – read on and you will find that you already know them and maybe didn't realise it.

How to make your basic unit

1 Mark out a piece of aluminium 20 swg (standard wire gauge) as shown in Figure 1a.

2 Cut, file and bend as shown (Fig. 1b).

3 Drill two pivot holes (Fig. 1c).

4 Cut and plane a simple beam (Fig. 1d).

5 Drill the beam (Fig. 1e).

6 Make a pivot peg (Fig. 1f).

7 Saw and plane the base (Fig. 1g).

8 Assemble the unit from bracket to base; fit the pivot peg and beam.

9.1: Getting to know the technical terms

Assemble your unit so that the rod runs through the centre hole of the beam (Fig. 2). This is the *fulcrum* or pivot point. Place a weight (nut) on the right-hand side (RHS). This we will call *load*. The beam will now tilt RHS down; to make it balance you have to push down on the left-hand side (LHS). The work you have applied we will call the *effort*. (Note: Another nut of the same weight and similar position would also have balanced the beam.) Does this remind you of something? Of course, a see-saw!

Now assemble your unit so the pivot rod (fulcrum) passes through the end hole (Fig. 3). Place a weight (load) in the middle of the beam. Where do you have to lift (apply effort to) the beam to make it horizontal? On the other end, of course! Can you think where this principle may be used? Possibly in a wheelbarrow!

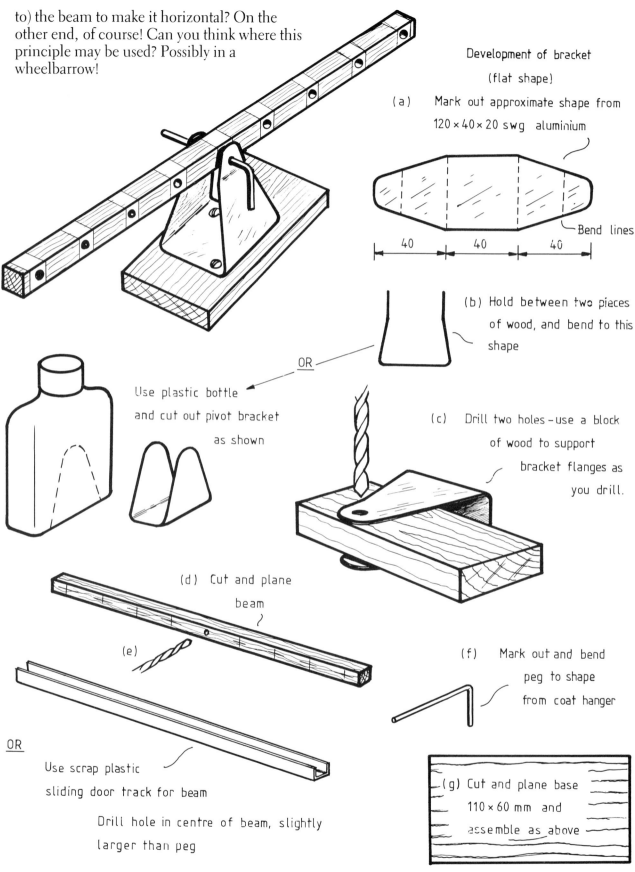

Development of bracket

(flat shape)

(a) Mark out approximate shape from 120 × 40 × 20 swg aluminium

Bend lines

40 40 40

(b) Hold between two pieces of wood, and bend to this shape

OR

Use plastic bottle and cut out pivot bracket as shown

(c) Drill two holes – use a block of wood to support bracket flanges as you drill.

(d) Cut and plane beam

(e)

(f) Mark out and bend peg to shape from coat hanger

OR

Use scrap plastic sliding door track for beam

Drill hole in centre of beam, slightly larger than peg

(g) Cut and plane base 110 × 60 mm and assemble as above

Fig. 1 The basic unit

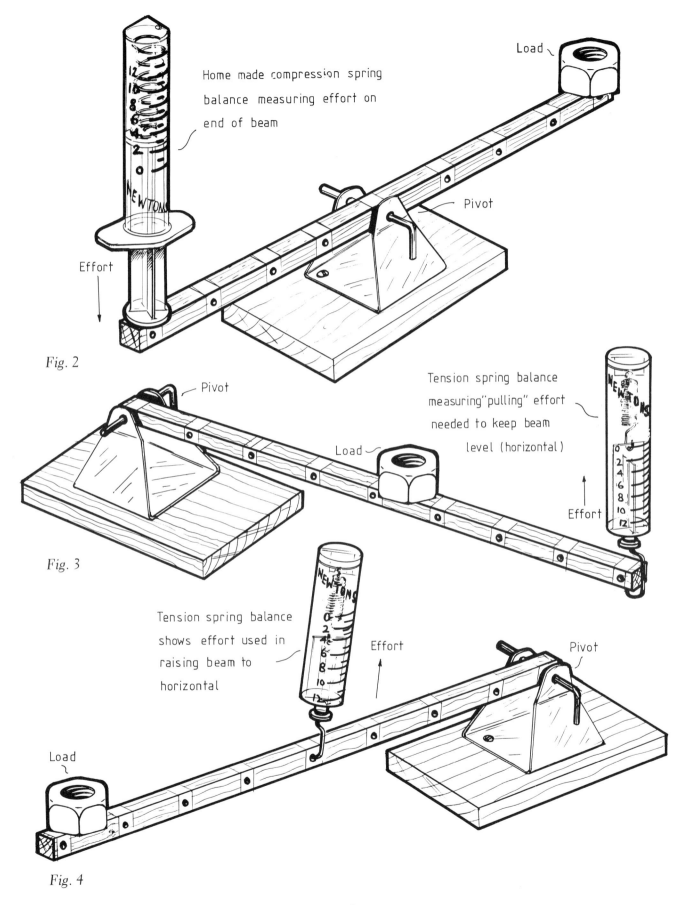

Home made compression spring balance measuring effort on end of beam

Load

Pivot

Effort

Fig. 2

Pivot

Tension spring balance measuring "pulling" effort needed to keep beam level (horizontal)

Load

Effort

Fig. 3

Tension spring balance shows effort used in raising beam to horizontal

Effort

Pivot

Load

Fig. 4

Now change the load and effort to that in Figure 4. What can you think of that has to be lifted (have effort applied) in the middle, the weight (load) on one end, and pivoted on the other? Answer – a spade. What else can you think of that this principle applies to?

Things to do and to find out

When you use your 'unit' as a see-saw:

1 You can only guess at the effort you have to apply. Use a spring balance to measure the effort and record the readings you obtain.

2 Each of the levers works differently. Make a sketch to show how each works.

3 Use known weights (weigh the nuts) to help you work out the results for step 2 above.

4 Select various tools, scissors etc. and show where the fulcrum (pivot), loads and efforts apply.

5 Define the term *fulcrum*.

NOTE

Turn to Briefs 14.1 and 14.2 to see how to make a spring balance using compression and tension. Use them in your experiments.

6 Explain the changes you found in the readings of the balances and the different types of levers shown.

9.2: Beatabalance

Now for some fun – see if you can outguess your friend. Let us use the first beam with the pivot (fulcrum) in the centre (Fig. 5). For weights you can still use nuts – provided they are the same size. A single weight has been placed above the third hole each side of the centre pivot. The beam should be in balance (equilibrium). The rule to balance the beam is: the weight × distance on the LHS must equal the weight × distance on the RHS.

You can also split the weights (Fig. 6). Try placing two weights above hole 4 on the LHS, which means the total on the LHS is $2 \times 4 = 8$. We can balance this out on the RHS by placing a single weight above hole 1, hole 3 and hole 4. Each weight and distance from the centre pivot is added to the other weights, i.e. $(1 \times 1) + (1 \times 3) + (1 \times 4) = 8$. The beam will balance! Note, however, that there are other solutions.

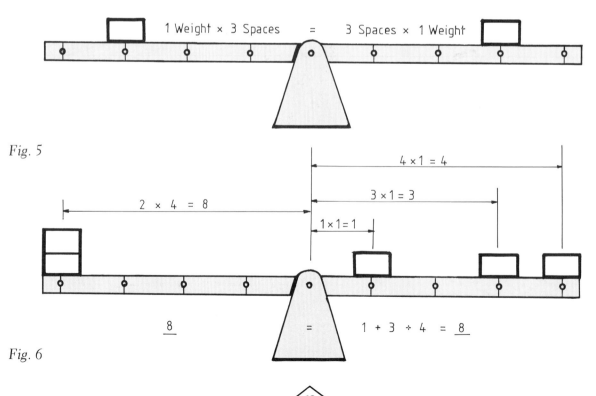

Fig. 5

Fig. 6

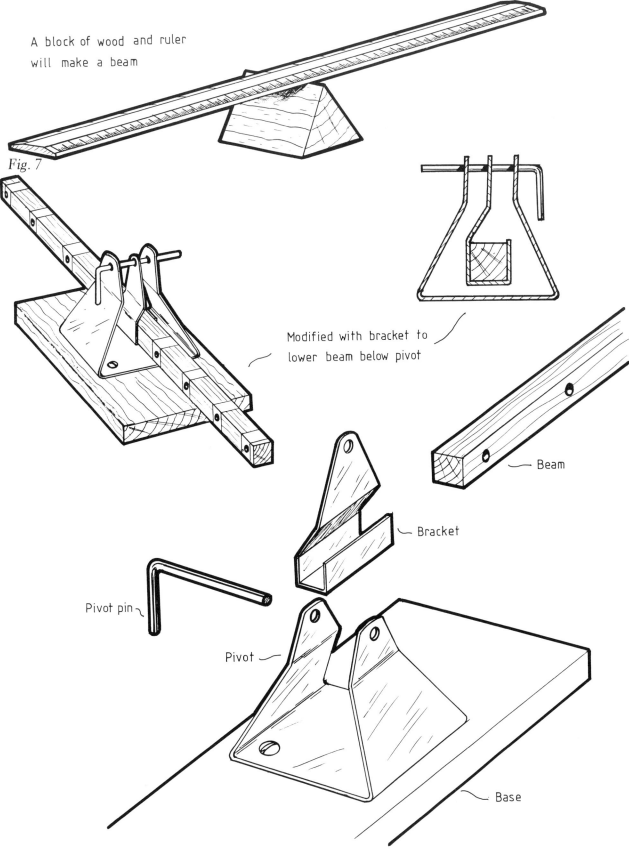

A block of wood and ruler
will make a beam

Fig. 7

Modified with bracket to
lower beam below pivot

Beam

Bracket

Pivot pin

Pivot

Base

Fig. 8

Brief

Using a Beatabalance, set a balancing problem to a friend by placing weights on the LHS. He/she must balance the beam on the RHS – but must not use the same settings as you did.

Rules

1 Set a time limit.

2 No guessing allowed – work it out!

3 Make it as complicated as you like.

Things to do and to find out

1 What else could you use as weights?

2 One problem is the sensitivity of the unit – a better-pivoted beam is possible (Fig. 7 and Photo 2).

3 Use other materials for the bracket and beam.

4 Can you use a fulcrum instead of a pivot? (Large hint!)

5 What is the smallest weight that the beam can measure?

6 The basic Beatabalance unit has a major design fault. Can *you* as a designer see why? Turn to Figure 8 and try to explain the problem with the earlier balance, compared with the one shown in the diagram.

Photo 2

9.3 Reaction tester (or a game of five stones)

Structures have to withstand different types of forces and loads (Photo 3). Two of these are the static (fixed) or dynamic (moving) loads, e.g. a car that is still or in motion. The foundations of a bridge have to support the weight of the bridge pushing (compressing) down. But they also have to withstand the forces acting on the bridge such as winds, moving vehicles and possibly a river and its moving current.

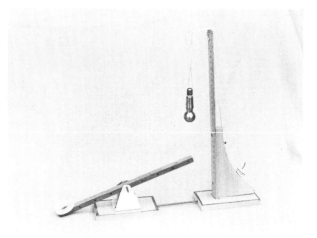

Photo 3

You may be able to sit carefully on a balloon and it will support your weight. You are a *static* load (Fig. 9). If you were to jump up and sit down quickly, the balloon would burst (Fig. 10). Your weight didn't change – but the way you applied it did. You changed the static load into a dynamic load and thus increased the force applied. The balloon was not designed to take this extra force and so it burst.

If you carry a heavy load on your back, after some time you get tired, you lose the energy to support it and you have to put it down. But you were only carrying a static load. If the same load is thrown onto your back, you would no doubt collapse. Your structure is not designed for these 'external' forces. The weight of the load remained the same, but by being thrown it was changed into a dynamic force.

Perhaps you can now see that building bridges or any other structure is not as easy as it first appears.

Fig. 9 A static *load*

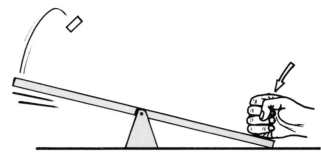

Fig. 11

Fig. 10 A dynamic (*moving*) load

9.4 Counterbalancing

This unit can be used to show how the weight of the structure of the unit can affect performance (Photos 4 and 5).

The following photographs are of projects designed by pupils using the basic unit as a starter. Sketch an 'exploded' view of the Human Cannonball (Photo 11) and the parts used in its construction. Turn to page 67 and see how well you have done.

Photo 4

Photo 5

Things to do and to find out

1 Using the unit, set the pivot rod through the centre hole and place a bottle-top or a weight on one end of the beam. With your hand, 'smack' the other end to shoot the top into the air. The harder you smack, the higher it goes (Fig. 11).

2 Move the pivot along a few places and place the top on the longer length of the beam (lever). Now hit the short end. Does moving the beam cause a change? Why?

3 Study Photo 3 and devise a way to measure the reactions that occur using this unit.

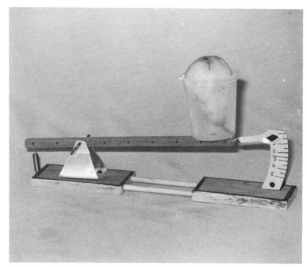

Photo 6

Photo 7

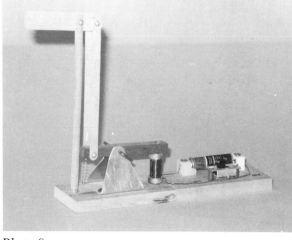

Photo 8

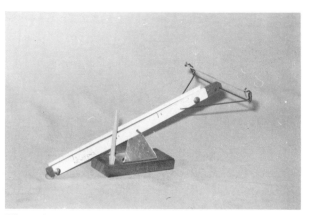

Photo 9

Photo 10

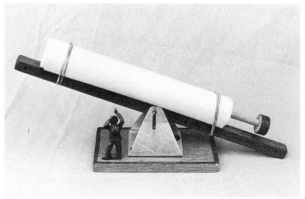

Photo 11

9.5 Ballista

Now you can see what we've been leading up to! All the previous Brainstormers show all the ideas and concepts necessary to design a ballista (Photo 12). You can still use the basic unit or start afresh!

"HUMAN CANNONBALL"

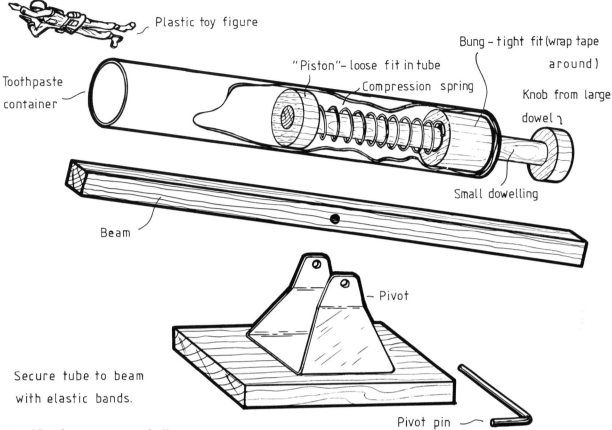

Plastic toy figure

"Piston"– loose fit in tube

Compression spring

Bung – tight fit (wrap tape around)

Toothpaste container

Knob from large dowel

Small dowelling

Beam

Pivot

Secure tube to beam with elastic bands.

Pivot pin

Fig. 12 *A human cannonball*

Brief

Design a ballista to project a ping-pong ball or another suitable object over a distance of 5 metres.

Photo 12

Things to do and to find out

1 How are you going to hold the ball or object in place?

2 In what positions will you have to place the pivot and why?

3 How will you stop the ballista's arm at the correct point to launch the ball?

4 How can you accurately measure the energy to launch?

5 How can you increase the energy?

6 Sketch your ideas to launch the ball.

7 Produce a target to aim at.

8 Use different materials to improve your ballista.

9 Produce a ballista that can be assembled
and dismantled.

10 Change your launcher to project a missile
with a rubber sucker on the end.

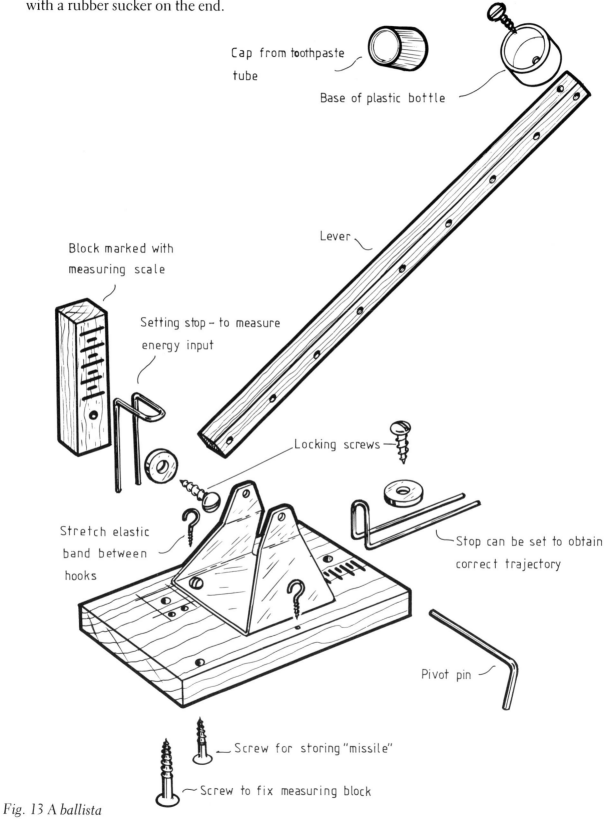

Cap from toothpaste tube

Base of plastic bottle

Lever

Block marked with measuring scale

Setting stop – to measure energy input

Locking screws

Stretch elastic band between hooks

Stop can be set to obtain correct trajectory

Pivot pin

Screw for storing "missile"

Screw to fix measuring block

Fig. 13 A ballista

ROLLABUGGY

Introduction

Brief

Design a forward-moving, backward-moving, steerable, speed-selecting, hand-operated, electrically-controlled vehicle for less than the cost of hiring a video cassette.

Impossible, you say! Not true. You can do just that in this section. The brief sounds impossible, but if *you* as the designer use the 'design process', it will be quite simple. What do we mean by the 'design process'? You have been using this all your life without knowing it! It is practical problem-solving in a logical way.

Let us reduce the difficult brief above to a number of smaller, simpler ones. The problems can be separated into the following areas: electrical motors, single switches, two-wheeled buggies, battery holders, two-way switching, steerability.

Brief 10.1

Design a simple Rollabuggy powered by an electric motor (Photo 1).

Photo 1

Problems arising include the following:
1 Choosing materials.
2 The sort of structure necessary to support the roller.
3 What mechanisms are possible.
4 What electrical circuit is required.
5 How the energy to drive the vehicle is going to be provided.
6 What size the buggy will need to be.
7 How much the materials will cost.
8 How long it will take to make.
9 How the efficiency of the buggy can be improved etc.

A designer puts his or her ideas on paper, makes notes and attempts to ask all those questions necessary to help solve the problem. Finally the designer chooses the best solution. Trial and error and a good deal of experiment and experience is often necessary to obtain a really good design.

You can try out this process in the next few briefs. Some guidance is given, but remember to try out ideas of your own. They may not all work, but quite often you learn a great deal from unsuccessful tests. You will certainly find out what is good and bad design.

Let us look at one way of tackling problems. Figure 1 shows a simple Rollabuggy.

Problem 1: What can you use as a roller?
Solution: Use a can or plastic bottle that has a hole drilled in each end for an axle to pass through.

Problem 2: What size hole for the axle?
Solution: Slightly larger diameter than the axle to ensure a running (bearing) fit.

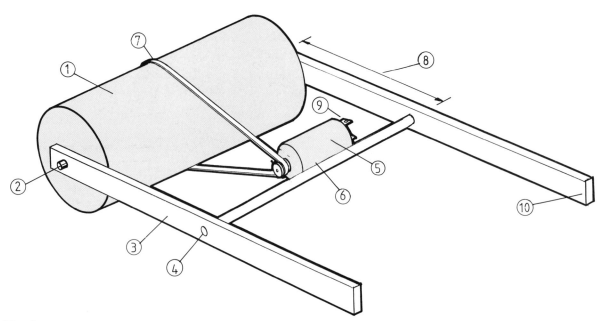

Fig. 1

Problem 3: What structure is required for the Rollabuggy?

Solution: Two side rails and an axle.

Problem 4: How will the axle be fitted to the rail?

Solution: Drill holes of a slightly smaller diameter than the axle to ensure a tight (interference) fit.

Problem 5: Where will you get a motor?

Solution: Discarded or broken toys at home, local model shop or teacher.

Problem 6: How will the motor be fitted to the Rollabuggy?

Solution: Use a second rod or rail to span the side rails and tape or glue the motor to it.

Problem 7: How can the Rollabuggy be driven by the motor?

Solution: Belt drive – elastic band around motor shaft and can. Size by trial and error.

Problem 8: How far apart will can and motor need to be?

Solution: As problem 7, although sewing (shirring) elastic may be the answer.

Problem 9: What circuit is needed and how will the battery be connected to the buggy?

Solution: Design a battery holder to fit into the Rollabuggy – but for this first experiment use long leads and just 'swop' connections to prove the basic idea.

Problem 10: Rails drag on ground (sliding friction).

Solution: Move on to the next brief.

Notice how each little problem is put in the form of a question. This is a very useful way of analysing (examining) a given brief.

Brief 10.2

Design a Rollabuggy to reduce sliding friction.

This problem arose because of the excess (non-useful) friction occurring when the rails dragged along the ground, reducing its efficiency. By including a further roller, wheel or wheels the friction is reduced considerably. Figure 2 shows various ideas, although in this

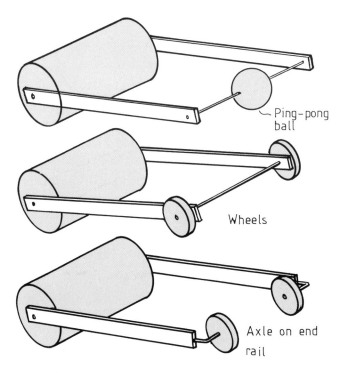

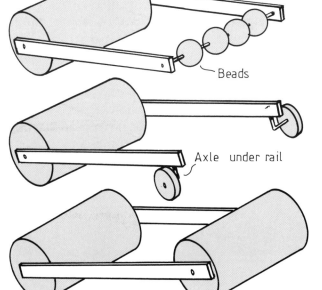

Ping-pong ball

Beads

Wheels

Axle under rail

Axle on end rail

Another can

Fig. 2

brief we are going to use another can for the second roller.

Things to do and to find out

Having reduced the sliding (non-useful) friction, you will need to increase the rolling (useful) friction to make your Rollabuggy more efficient – particularly if you try to make it climb a slight slope (gradient).

1 Experiment by using a band as shown in Figure 3.

2 Suggest other ways of increasing friction.

3 Explain the difference between useful and non-useful friction.

Brief 10.3

Design a battery holder for your Rolla-buggy (Photo 2).

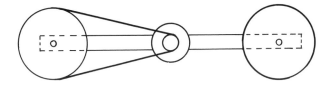

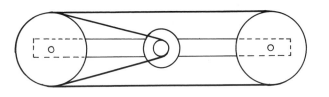

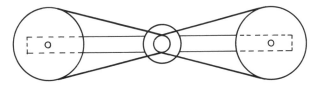

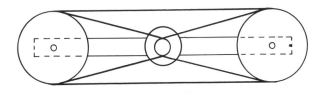

Fig. 3

A means of fixing a battery to your Rollabuggy is necessary. A single cell (battery) of 1.5 volts works well. A battery of a larger voltage may produce too much energy. Small motors will usually work up to 6 V – but check them carefully, as any higher voltage could damage your motor.

Two ideas are shown in Figures 4 and 5. One clips onto a strap or bracket and is therefore detachable. The other is adjustable for either one or two cells, but is a more permanent design.

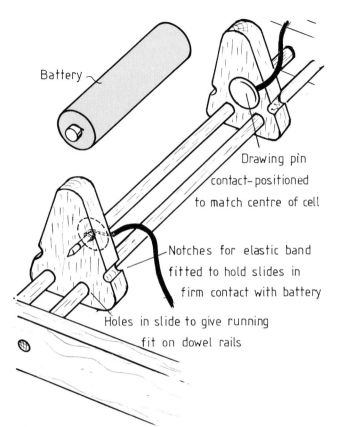

Fig. 5

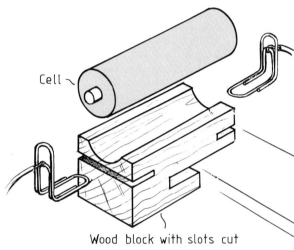

Wood block with slots cut
for paperclips to be pushed in
with tight fit

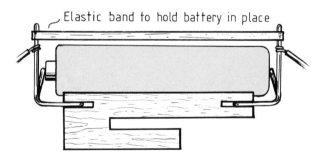

Fig. 4

1 The device in Figure 4 can be fitted to a flat plate. Modify the design so it can be fitted to (a) the rod (b) the rail.

2 Design a holder so it can be used vertically.

3 Paper clips are a weakness of this holder. Improve on the idea.

4 Make a holder from a different material.

5 The design in Figure 5 is built into the vehicle. Modify (change) the design to use (a) two cells (b) a 4.5 V flat battery.

6 Think of a simple way to prevent the batteries from coming out of position.

7 What size will the holder need to be?

8 How can you improve the contacts for the battery connections?

9 List other problems that occur in making your model. How can you overcome them?

SAFETY NOTE

Slide a piece of card between each paper clip. This will prevent a short circuit, should the insulation around the rim of the battery get damaged (Fig. 6).

Fig. 6

Photo 2

Brief 10.4

Design a single switch for your Rolla-buggy to control starting and stopping (Photo 2).

You can have some fun with the buggy, but it can be frustrating having to pick it up in order to disconnect wires and clips. There is a way you can easily put a hand-operated switch on to your vehicle. This uses the principle (idea) of an elastic band and lever that is made to spring past a 'neutral' position, causing the buggy to start or stop.

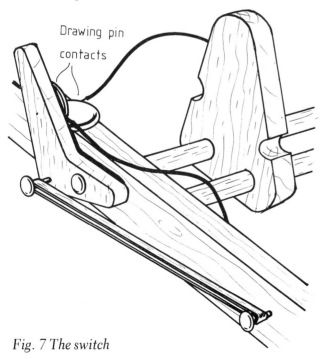

Drawing pin contacts

Fig. 7 The switch

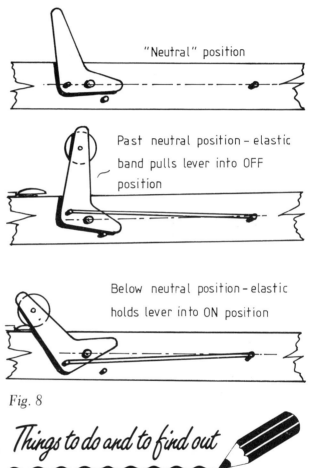

"Neutral" position

Past neutral position – elastic band pulls lever into OFF position

Below neutral position – elastic holds lever into ON position

Fig. 8

Things to do and to find out

1 Make a switch with a longer lever – for ease of operating (Fig. 7).

2 Use materials other than those shown.

3 The pin holding the lever is the fulcrum, the panel pin on the lever is the load, and the band hooked over the pin in the rail is the effort. If the panel pins are not in line, the energy in the band will pull the lever past the 'neutral point', either completing or opening the circuit (see Fig. 8).

4 Find out by experiment the best position for the pins.

5 In what other ways can you fix the lever to the rail? Remember: it must move easily.

6 Think of other ways of connecting the circuit and switches. There are plenty of them!

Brief 10.5

Design a two-way switch so that you can control the Rollabuggy in forward and reverse direction, and at a chosen speed.

The next improvement to the Rollabuggy is to make it go forward and in reverse. To do this we need to change the single switch into a two-way type. In some houses there are two switches for a single light; for instance you can turn a light on downstairs and then turn it off upstairs. A similar type of switch is required here. It would also help if the weight of the vehicle could be reduced. We can do this by designing a hand-held switch and possibly the battery as well. A rheostat can be used to control the speed of your motor (see Brief 16).

How to make your two way switch
(Fig. 9 and Photo 3)

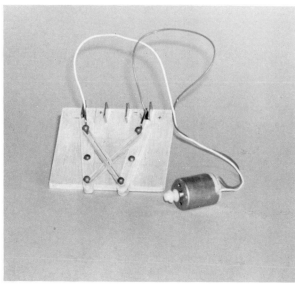

Photo 3

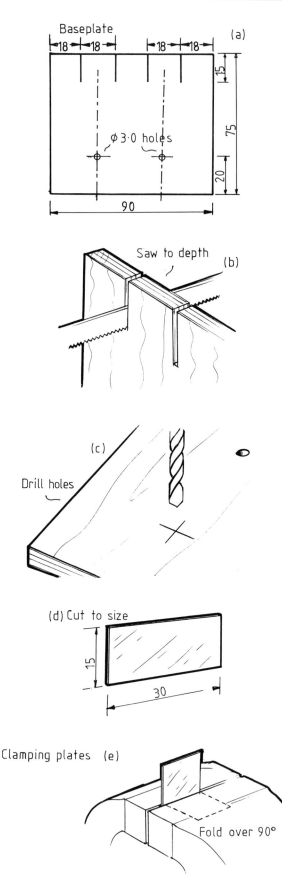

Fig. 9 The two-way switch

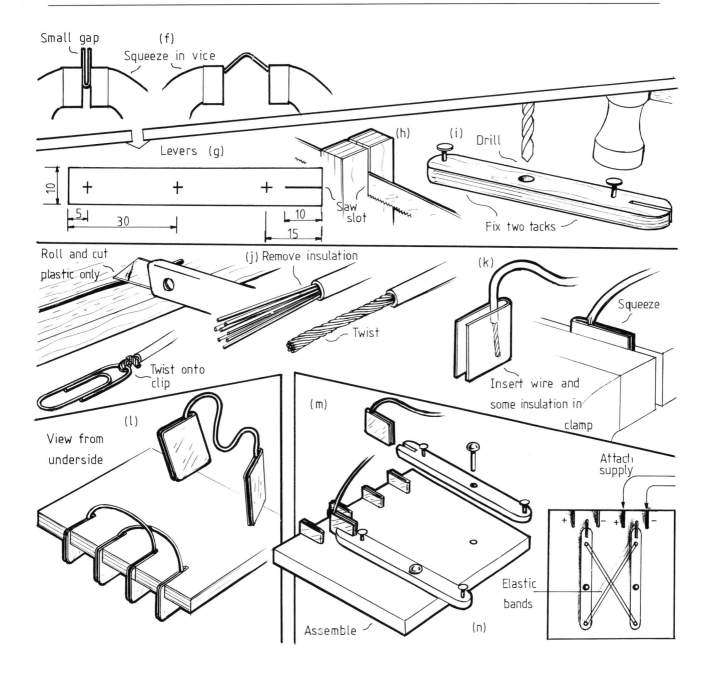

Small gap (f) Squeeze in vice

Levers (g)

10

5 30 10 15

Saw slot

(h) (i) Drill

Fix two tacks

Roll and cut plastic only

(j) Remove insulation

Twist

Twist onto clip

(k)

Squeeze

Insert wire and some insulation in clamp

(l)

View from underside

(m)

Attach supply

Elastic bands

Assemble (n)

Board

1 Mark out the dimensions as shown in Figure 9a on a piece of 6 mm plywood.

2 Saw four slots in the board with a hacksaw to a depth of 15 mm (Fig. 9b).

3 Drill the two ∅ 3.0 mm holes (Fig. 9c).

Clamping plates for board

1 Mark out four plates 30 mm × 15 mm from thin sheet metal.

2 Saw, file and deburr to size (Fig. 9d).

3 Place in vice and fold 90° at centre (Fig. 9e).

4 Reposition in vice and squeeze gently – leaving a slight gap! (Fig. 9f).

NOTE

The wire is going to be clamped between the plates – it is assumed you have no soldering equipment at home. However, soldering is a better method and this is shown later.

Levers

1 Obtain two pieces of thin plywood 70 mm × 10 mm in size.

2 Mark out as shown in Figure 9g.

3 Saw slot 10 mm in depth (Fig. 9h).

4 Drill hole to suit rivet ∅ 3.2 mm (Fig. 9i).

5 Tap small tacks into board.

NOTE

For appearance the levers can be shaped prior to fixing panel pins (Fig. 9i).

Clamp plates for levers

1 Mark out, cut and file to size two pieces of thin sheet metal 30 mm × 10 mm.

2 Repeat the previous stages as for the board clamping plates.

Wiring the board

1 Decide on the length of wire required from your hand-control board to the Rollabuggy on the ground. Cut off two pieces.

2 Remove the plastic covering (insulation) from the ends of each wire (Fig. 9j).

3 Assemble one end of each wire to the lever clamp plates (Fig. 9k).

4 Attach the other end of each wire to a paper clip or crocodile clip. The paper clips are a simple way of attaching wires to plates or electrical connections. However, they are not always a well-made connection, and it can be frustrating to have a poor contact in your circuit. A crocodile clip will remove this problem.

5 The clips are ready to be attached to the motor of your Rollabuggy.

6 Cut two pieces of wire of length 60 mm.

7 Strip ends as described earlier.

8 Attach wires to the board clamping plates (Fig. 9l).

9 Assemble plates to the board (Fig. 9m). The slot may need to be 'opened out' to take the plate. By using a saw you can make this slot wide enough to ensure a tight fit. Practise on a scrap piece of wood first!

Assembly of levers to board

1 The holes in the board are of ∅ 3 mm and the holes in the levers are of ∅ 3.2 mm. Using a rivet of ∅ 3.2 mm push this through the lever and 'press' the rivet into the board. It should give a nice action on your lever and yet the lever will remain fixed to the board (Fig. 9).

2 Attach the rubber bands and mark the positive (+ VE) and negative (− VE) connections of the battery supply.

Soldering – safety rules

1 Always use a stand for the soldering iron.

2 Use a damp sponge to clean the end of the iron.

3 'Tin' each item to be soldered and solder items together.

NOTE

A flux paste is necessary if electricians' solder is not used.

4 Do not touch the end of the iron or allow the end of the soldering iron to touch its own lead.

NOTE

'Tin' or 'tinning' means applying a thin layer of solder before assembling electrical items.

Brief 10.6

> Design a method of steering your Rolla-buggy (Photo 4).

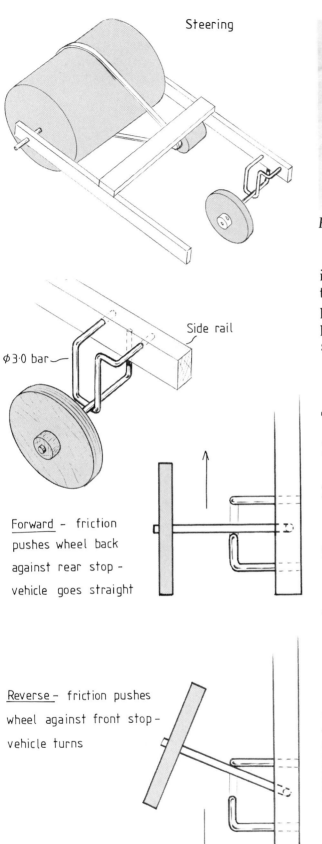

Steering

Side rail

φ3·0 bar

Forward - friction
pushes wheel back
against rear stop -
vehicle goes straight

Reverse - friction pushes
wheel against front stop -
vehicle turns

Fig. 10

Photo 4

We have now reached the last stage of that initial brief. You can see that by working through a brief in stages and solving each small problem in turn it becomes easier to solve the problem as a whole. One way of solving the steering problem is shown in Figure 10.

Things to do and to find out

1 Decide whether you want front- or rear-wheel steering.

2 The axle of the wheel is bent through 90° and fitted into the rail. What size hole must this be?

3 You may need to drill a 'blind' hole (one that does not go all the way through the rail). Explain why this may be necessary.

4 How can you increase the friction of the steering wheel?

5 Improve the method shown of stop adjustment for the steering.

Brief 10.7

Measure the speed (revolutions per minute or r.p.m.) of your motor.

It is often necessary to find out the speed of a motor and reduce it or increase it. Drilling machines need to be speed-controlled and we achieve this using pulleys and belts. We know how to control the motor speed, but have not yet found out just how fast the motor shaft is turning.

How to find out the speed (in r.p.m.) of the motor shaft (example).

1 Use a small 1.5 V cell (HP 7).

2 Measure the diameter of the can.

3 Measure the diameter of the motor shaft.

4 This will give you a *ratio* (comparison of one diameter with another), e.g. Ø 64 mm to Ø 2 mm – we reduce this to 32:1.

5 Hold the Rollabuggy in your hand, mark the can and switch on. Count the turns of the can for 30 seconds.

6 As we want revolutions per minute, multiply by 2.

7 We now have a figure of $45 \times 2 = 90$.

8 If the diameter of the can is 32 times larger than the diameter of the small shaft and its speed per minute is 90, multiplying the two together will give us the speed of the motor $= 32 \times 90 = 2880$ r.p.m.

Things to do and to find out

1 Try out this procedure with your motor.

2 Race your buggy against another and find out if the faster motor drives the faster buggy. Although you might expect this, sometimes it does not happen. Why not?

3 Increase the energy by using two cells – although this time the speed of the can may become difficult to count. Why is this?

4 Your test may produce some inaccurate readings. Why is this so and what might you do to improve them?

5 Try the vehicle along the ground and check whether the results are the same as those you obtained when you held it in the hand.

Brief 10.8

Convert your Rollabuggy into a winch.

The Rollabuggy is clamped so that it overhangs a bench. A line is attached to the roller, separate from the motor belt. When the motor is operated, the rotary motion is changed and *linear* motion takes place. We can therefore raise or lower whatever is on the end of the line. Perhaps you can see how the concept (idea) is used in a mine shaft to raise and lower the cage.

An example of a winch is given in Figure 11a.

Things to do and to find out

1 Place a separate line over each roller, add equal weights and switch on the supply. There will be a difference in the speed of the weights being raised. Why is this?

2 Work out the ratio of each roller to the motor.

3 Set the large roller (pulley) to rotate freely. With your spring tension balance and a weight of 4 newtons, assemble the equipment as shown in Figure 11b.

4 Pull the balance, lift the weight and record your observations. Why does the tension balance measure a greater *force* than the weight (load) being lifted? What causes this extra force? Why should you repeat this experiment more than once?

5 When you used the balance and raised the weight, you carried out *work*. We can find out the amount of work applied by recording results and placing them into a formula. Record:
   (a) the *distance* the weight was raised, e.g. 1 metre.
   (b) the amount of *force* (in newtons) necessary to lift it, e.g. 4 newtons.
The formula is:
work done = force × distance
work done = 4 × 1 (substituting readings from (a) and (b))
work done = 4 newton metres or 4 Nm

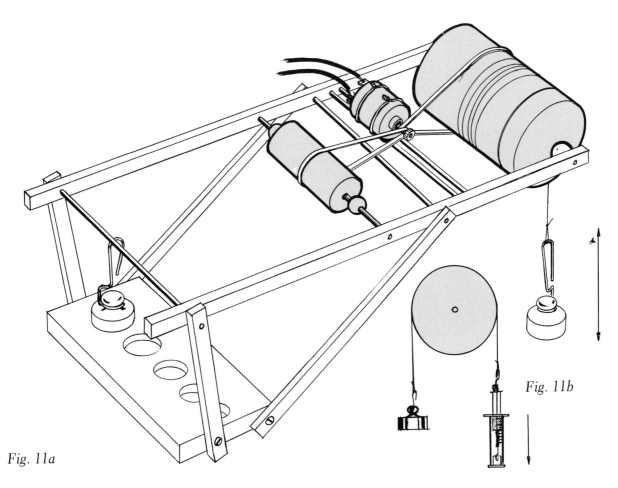

Fig. 11a

Fig. 11b

6 Let us now find out the time (in seconds) taken to raise the weight through a distance of 1 metre. Assume it took 4 seconds to move 1 metre. Therefore for 1 second it will take ¼ or 0.25 m/s (0.25 metres per second).

7 Now we know the time taken to raise the load in 1 second we can find out the *power output*. The formula is:

power output = $\dfrac{\text{work done}}{\text{time taken}}$

= $\dfrac{4 \text{ Nm}}{4 \text{s}}$ (substituting from steps 5 and 6)

= 1 Nm/s

NOTE

1 Nm/s is equal to 1 watt (the electrical unit of power).

8 We can now find out the *power input*. The formula is: power input = volts × amps.
Connect a 1.5 volt battery to our winch, measure the *amperage* across the motor

terminals as the winch is being used (ask your teacher to demonstrate the *ammeter* to you). Let us assume you obtained a reading of 2 amps.

power input = volts × amps

= 1.5 × 2 (substituting from above)

= 3 W (3 watts)

9 Finally we can find out the *efficiency* of our winch. The formula is:

efficiency = $\dfrac{\text{power output}}{\text{power input}} \times \dfrac{100}{1}$

= $\dfrac{1}{3} \times \dfrac{100}{1}$ (substituting from steps 7 and 8)

= 33⅓%

10 Construct your own winch and try to work out the work done, time taken, power output, power input and efficiency of your design.

11 Use the knowledge gained here and apply it to your Rollabuggy.

BOATS

Introduction

There are many types of boats and ships. Tankers, aircraft carriers, battleships, rowing boats and speedboats, canoes and paddleboats. They have all been designed for a particular purpose. You may have seen competitions of raft races. These rafts have been constructed from materials such as empty oil drums, plastic bags filled with air, planks of wood – indeed, anything that floats!

Some ideas are more successful than others. Let us look at ways to design and propel a boat. However, *don't forget* that the ideas shown are only examples! Try them and improve on them by choosing better materials or designing a better method of construction.

Photo 1

Brief 11.1

Design a paddleboat using an elastic band for power (Photo 1).

This is one of the quickest and easiest boats to make. Almost any material from a plastic container to a piece of wood could be suitable for the hull (floats) of the boat. An example is shown in Figure 1 and this hull is used in other briefs to show how a basic part (a component) can be used and ideas developed around it.

How to make paddle boat

1 Cut two pieces of material to size and shape the ends to suit (Fig. 1a).

2 Drill three holes in each hull piece.

3 Cut two pieces of dowel to fit the hulls together.

4 Assemble the structure for the paddleboat (Fig. 1b).

Paddle
1 Mark out and cut two pieces of thin ply or laminate to size (Fig. 1c).

2 Cut a slot in each.

3 Assemble it by sliding the pieces together (Fig. 1d).

4 Loop an elastic band around the paddle (Fig. 1e).

5 Attach the bands to the paddleboat (Fig. 1f).

6 Wind up (energise) the paddleboat (Fig. 1g).

PADDLE BOAT

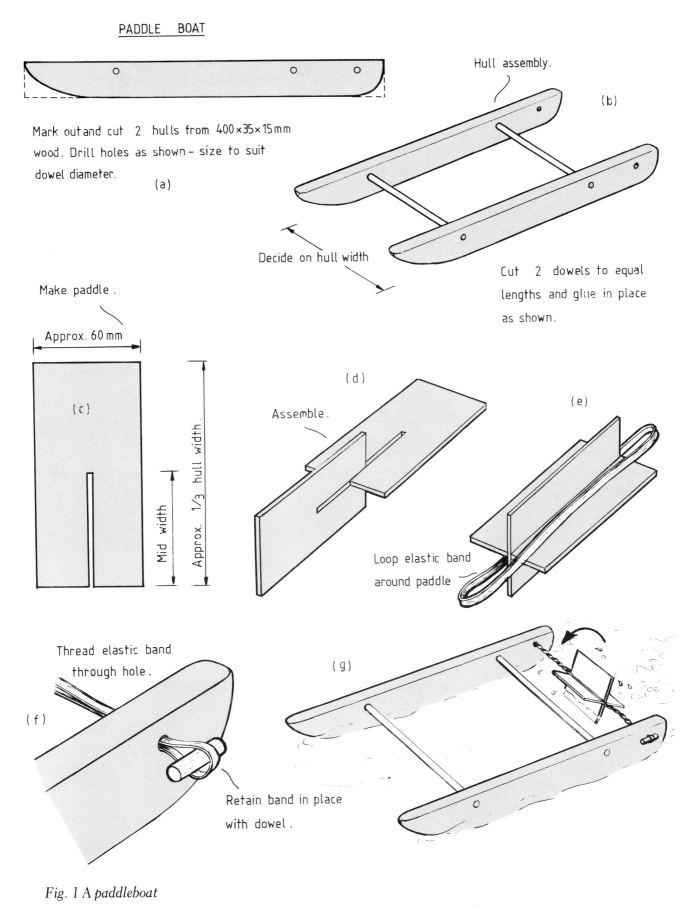

Mark out and cut 2 hulls from 400×35×15mm wood. Drill holes as shown – size to suit dowel diameter.

(a)

Hull assembly.

(b)

Decide on hull width

Cut 2 dowels to equal lengths and glue in place as shown.

Make paddle.

Approx. 60 mm

(c)

Mid width

Approx. ⅓ hull width.

Assemble.

(d)

(e)

Loop elastic band around paddle

Thread elastic band through hole.

(f)

(g)

Retain band in place with dowel.

Fig. 1 A paddleboat

Things to do and to find out

1 Alter the size of the paddle and explain any changes in the performance.

2 If your floats are light, you may find the front of the boat lifts out of the water. Why is this?

3 Try operating the boat with the paddle at the front and explain whether this eliminates the lifting.

4 Fix two paddles to your boat, front and rear. How does this affect the performance?

5 Vary the energy powering the boat by changing or increasing the number of elastic bands. Make a table to show how these change the boat's performance. Use fifty turns on each band first of all.

6 In what other ways can you attach the elastic band(s) to the boat?

7 Design different-shaped hulls (floats). Find out if this affects performance.

8 Why do some floats sink deeper into the water than others?

9 Design a colour scheme for your boat. What sort of paints are best to decorate it?

10 Try to get your paddleboat to go as far as possible – but as slowly as possible.

11 Include extra blades on your paddle. What is their effect?

12 Describe the difference in performance between short-depth paddle blades and long-depth paddle blades.

13 The reason the floats lift out of the water is due to *torque* – explain how torque is produced.

Brief 11.2

Design a scull-acting Floataboat (Photo 2).

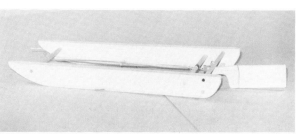

Photo 2

This design stems from nature in that it is simulating (copying) the tail action of a fish. A goldfish, for example, weaves (sculls) its tail from side to side to propel itself forward.

How to make the scull-acting boat (Fig. 2)

1 Make two floats as in the previous brief.

2 Drill three holes at the rear of the sculler (Fig. 2a).

3 Decide on the width of boat and drill one ∅ 1.5 mm hole through the centre of each dowel (Fig. 2b).

4 Assemble the scull-acting boat (Fig. 2c).

Paddle
1 Mark out, cut and shape the paddle to approximate size, from 3 mm jelutong or similar material (Fig. 2d).

2 Saw a thin slot in the end of paddle to take a metal flicker (Fig. 2e).

3 Make the flicker (Fig. 2f).

Crank and winder
1 Obtain two paper clips and straighten them out.

2 Shape the crank to size (Fig. 2g).

3 Solder the washer or glue the head to the crank.

4 Shape the winder (Fig. 2h).

5 Make the locating paddle-pin.

6 Drill a hole through the paddle to take the locating pin (Fig. 2i).

7 Assemble the boat (Fig. 2j).

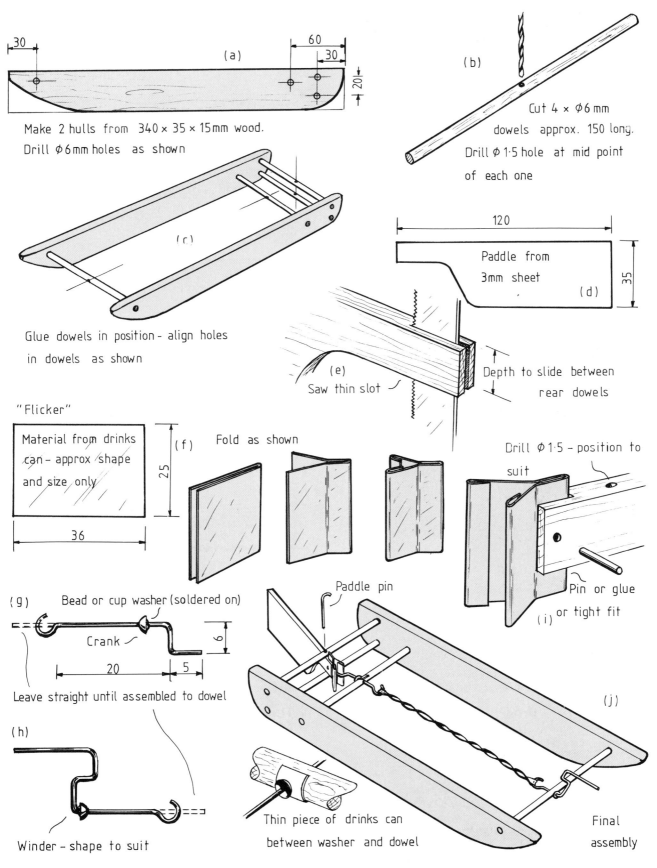

(a)

30   60   30   20

Make 2 hulls from 340 × 35 × 15mm wood.
Drill ⌀6mm holes as shown

(b)

Cut 4 × ⌀6mm
dowels approx. 150 long.
Drill ⌀1·5 hole at mid point
of each one

(c)

Glue dowels in position - align holes
in dowels as shown

120   35

Paddle from
3mm sheet   (d)

(e)
Saw thin slot

Depth to slide between
rear dowels

"Flicker"

Material from drinks
can - approx shape
and size only   (f)

25   36

Fold as shown

Drill ⌀1·5 - position to
suit

(i) or tight fit

Pin or glue

(g)   Bead or cup washer (soldered on)

Crank

6   20   5

Leave straight until assembled to dowel

Paddle pin

(j)

(h)

Winder - shape to suit

Thin piece of drinks can
between washer and dowel

Final
assembly

Fig. 2 A sculler

Things to do and to find out

1 What size will the paddle need to be to make your sculler work well?

2 Using elastic bands, how can you make it travel (a) slowly, (b) quickly?

3 How can you make the scull operate over a long period of time?

4 Where does friction affect the scull's performance?

5 Can you improve the scull by redesigning its structure?

6 Experiment with the angles of the flicker and state its effect.

7 Design a colour scheme for the scull.

8 Explain how the scull works – use short notes and sketches.

9 What are the minimum number of turns of the elastic band needed to make your scull move forward? Why is this?

10 Make a performance graph showing the number of turns plotted against distance travelled.

11 List the energy changes occurring when the scull is in use.

Brief 11.3

Design a propeller-driven Ski-boat (Photo 3).

Photo 3.

The previous two briefs used a form of paddle to propel the boat through the water. Let us now look at using the elastic band to drive a propeller that is *out* of the water.

How to make your ski-boat (Fig. 3)

1 Make one hull (float) as in Brief 11.1.

2 Cut two outside floats from an expanded polystyrene food tray (Fig. 3a).

3 Cut two wire struts $\varnothing$ 1.5 × 240 (Fig. 3b).

4 Mark out, shape and drill the propeller support (Fig. 3c).

5 Drill a hole in the propeller slightly larger than a paper clip.

6 Make a drive shaft for the propeller from a paper clip (Fig. 3d).

7 Cut four wooden blocks, glue and drill them.

8 Assemble the boat (Fig. 3e).

Things to do and to find out

1 How far apart do the floats need to be to balance the ski-boat?

2 What other materials or containers could you use for the floats?

3 Where is the best position for the struts of the floats?

4 How must the propeller be assembled and wound up?

5 How can you make the propeller rotate for a longer time?

6 Experiment to find out the best size and number of elastic bands for energising the boat.

7 Does the propeller size have any effect on performance?

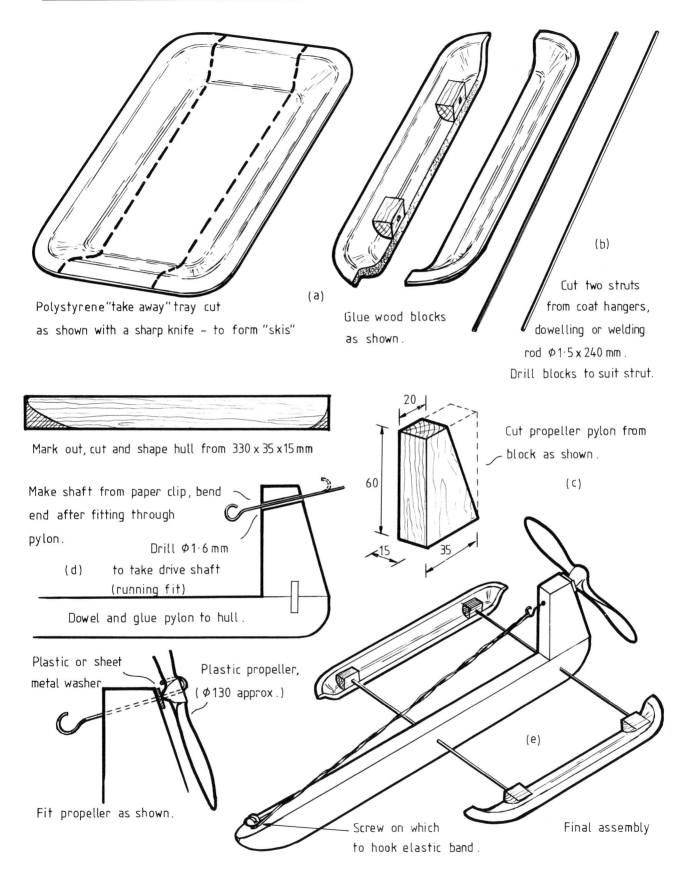

Polystyrene "take away" tray cut as shown with a sharp knife – to form "skis"

(a)

Glue wood blocks as shown.

(b)

Cut two struts from coat hangers, dowelling or welding rod φ1·5 x 240 mm. Drill blocks to suit strut.

Mark out, cut and shape hull from 330 x 35 x 15 mm

Make shaft from paper clip, bend end after fitting through pylon.

Drill φ1·6 mm

(d)   to take drive shaft (running fit)

Dowel and glue pylon to hull.

20

60

15   35

Cut propeller pylon from block as shown.

(c)

Plastic or sheet metal washer

Plastic propeller, (φ130 approx.)

Fit propeller as shown.

(e)

Screw on which to hook elastic band.

Final assembly

Fig. 3 A ski-boat

8 In a flow chart, show the energy changes which take place when the ski-boat is moving.

9 Make the largest and fastest ski-boat that you can. Choose your own materials and sizes to achieve this.

10 Design a colour scheme for your boat and paint it.

Brief 11.4

Design a candle-powered 'Pop-pop' boat (Photo 4).

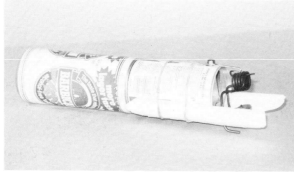

Photo 4

Solar power is used today in developing countries by means of the concept shown in this next project. There it is used as an energising source to pump water from the ground. We, however, are using heat from a candle flame as our energising source for the boat.

How to make the 'Pop-pop' boat
(Fig. 4)

1 Obtain two empty drinks cans.

2 Cut a piece of copper piping of I/D (internal diameter) Ø 1.0 mm and O/D (outside diameter) Ø 3.0 mm to a length of 500 mm.

Shaping the copper coil
(With care this can be done without any pre-heating.)

1 Place a Ø 20 bar in a vice with 100 mm protruding.

2 Rest the centre of the copper tube over the bar and commence 'wrapping' the tube around the bar (Fig. 4a). Try to form other bends required around a round bar of approximately Ø 12 (Fig. 4b).

3 Cut two floats from an expanded polystyrene food tray (see previous brief).

4 Make a bracket to support the candle (Fig. 4c).

5 Glue it to the drinks can – what adhesive will be best for this?

6 Make a clip for the coil (a curtain hook was used for the example) (Fig. 4d).

7 Fix the clip to the drinks can (Fig. 4e).

8 Place the floats in position (Fig. 4f).

9 Attach the coil.

10 Place a candle on the support bracket so that, when lit, the flame touches the coil.

NOTE

The coil will require 'priming'. That is, it needs to be filled with water before you float the 'Pop-pop' boat itself. Fill a plastic squeezy bottle with water, place the nozzle over one end of the coil tube and force the water into the coil until it comes out of the other end. Cover tube ends with your fingers and attach the coil to the boat.

Things to do and to find out

1 Try changing the diameter and length of the copper tubing. Does this improve the performance?

2 In the given brief you were instructed to obtain two cans. Why do you think this is necessary?

3 How can you make your 'Pop-pop' boat float higher in the water? (If it floats too low, the candle may be put out.)

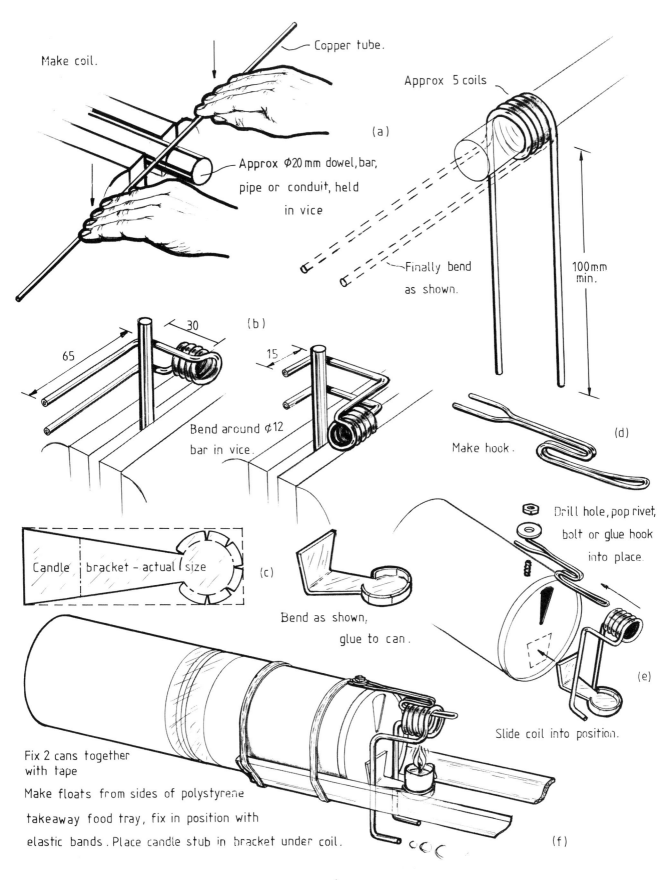

Make coil.

Copper tube.

Approx Ø20 mm dowel, bar, pipe or conduit, held in vice

Approx 5 coils

(a)

Finally bend as shown.

100mm min.

65

30

(b)

15

Bend around Ø12 bar in vice.

Make hook.

(d)

Candle | bracket – actual size

(c)

Bend as shown, glue to can.

Drill hole, pop rivet, bolt or glue hook into place.

(e)

Slide coil into position.

Fix 2 cans together with tape

Make floats from sides of polystyrene takeaway food tray, fix in position with elastic bands. Place candle stub in bracket under coil.

(f)

Fig. 4 A 'Pop-pop' boat

4 Carefully observe the action of the boat after lighting the candle. List the changes as it goes through its firing sequence.

5 The 'Pop-pop' boat will stop working and then restart – why is this?

6 Try to explain how the boat works. Some of the following terms may help: heat, steam, vacuum, suction, cooling.

Remember: a good technologist must have *patience* in experimenting. One tip is to list each change or experiment as you carry it out, so that you do not repeat it later on.

Design a different structure for your boat. Remember that this is only a starter project. The boat will take 30 seconds or so to start.

SAFETY NOTE

Do not touch the coil once the candle is lit, as it becomes very hot.

Brief 11.5

Design a sailboat to which you can add other components (Photo 5).

Photo 5

The above brief is just another way of using a basic shell or structure, that can have additional items added to it in order to change its design.

How to make the sailboat (Fig. 5)

1 Obtain two plastic containers with caps – to be used as floats.

2 Join the containers together (Fig. 5a).

3 Incorporate (include) a way of fixing a mast (Fig. 5b).

4 Make a mast and fit it. Choose a convenient shape and size for a sail. Cut one out of polythene film and fix it to the mast (Fig. 5c).

Things to do and to find out

1 Study books on sail boats to find out how to improve the method of attaching a sail.

2 Experiment to find out the best shape and size of sail for your hull.

3 Does your sailboat need a rudder for steering?

4 What other materials make a good sail?

5 How strong a wind is required to make your boat sail well?

6 Try using a vacuum cleaner or hair dryer to provide artificial wind to help you solve these problems.

7 Choose other materials to improve the sailboat's performance.

8 How can you make the sailboat 'sail' if no water tank is available? Move on to the next brief!

Brief 11.6

Change the sailboat design to that of a land yacht (Photo 6).

You may not have a convenient pool on which to sail your boat. So let us change the design to enable your sailboat to operate on land and water (an amphibious boat). This is very easily done, as in Figure 6.

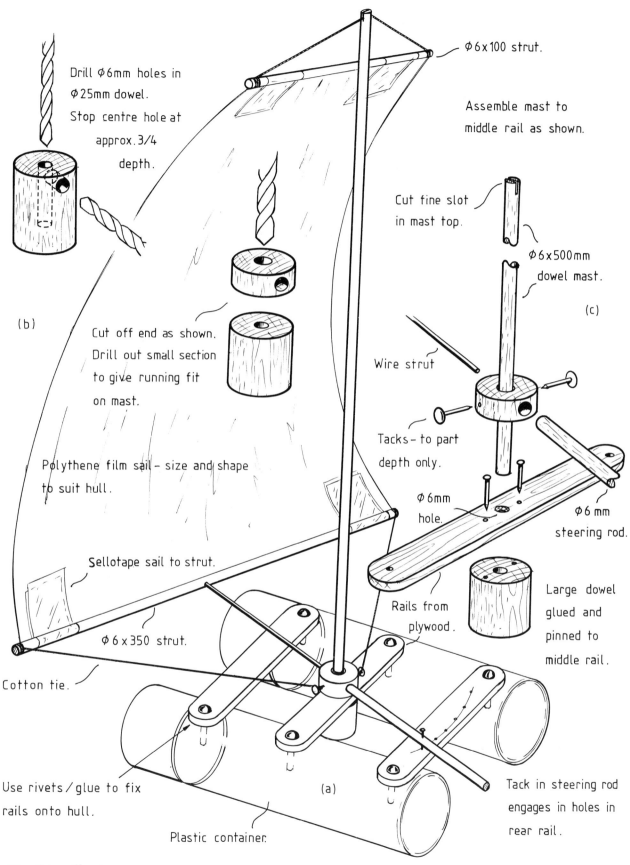

Drill ⌀6mm holes in
⌀25mm dowel.
Stop centre hole at
approx. 3/4
depth.

⌀6x100 strut.

Assemble mast to
middle rail as shown.

Cut fine slot
in mast top.

⌀6x500mm
dowel mast.

(c)

(b)

Cut off end as shown.
Drill out small section
to give running fit
on mast.

Wire strut

Tacks – to part
depth only.

⌀6mm
hole.

⌀6 mm
steering rod.

Polythene film sail – size and shape
to suit hull.

Rails from
plywood.

Large dowel
glued and
pinned to
middle rail.

Sellotape sail to strut.

⌀6 x 350 strut.

Cotton tie.

Use rivets / glue to fix
rails onto hull.

(a)

Tack in steering rod
engages in holes in
rear rail.

Plastic container.

Fig. 5 A sailboat

Photo 6

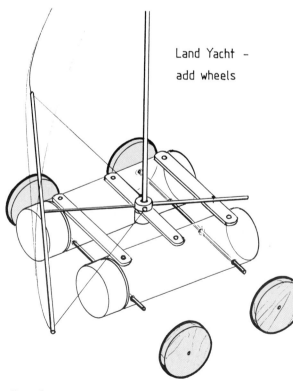

Land Yacht –
add wheels

Fig. 6

Things to do and to find out

1 Adding wheels will increase the weight of the boat. What effect does this have on the level at which it floats?

2 How can you overcome the problem of drilling holes for axles and yet prevent water from entering the container?

3 How will you mark out accurately the hole positions?

4 Try ways of reducing friction in your land yacht.

5 Compare the difference using three wheels instead of four on the land yacht.

6 Make the boat or land yacht self-propelling – move onto the next brief.

Brief 11.7

Design a self-propulsion unit for your sailboat or land yacht (Fig. 7).

You can have little fun with your sailboat or land yacht if there is no wind! Let us now add a motor and propeller to your unit (Photo 7).

How to make a self-propelled boat

Propeller and motor mount (Fig. 7a)

1 Make a motor bracket from thin sheet of metal 20 × 200 mm.

2 Cut a securing peg for the elastic band using Ø 3.0 × 100 mild steel rod.

3 Fix the propeller to the motor.

4 Solder the leads to the motor.

5 Make slide mounts from wood 8 mm × 25 mm × 25 mm.

6 Make a battery holder from thin sheet metal
100 × 50 (Fig. 7b).

NOTE

Make the centre V of the bracket large enough
to hold the motor.

7 Assemble the power unit to the hull and test
it (Fig. 7c).

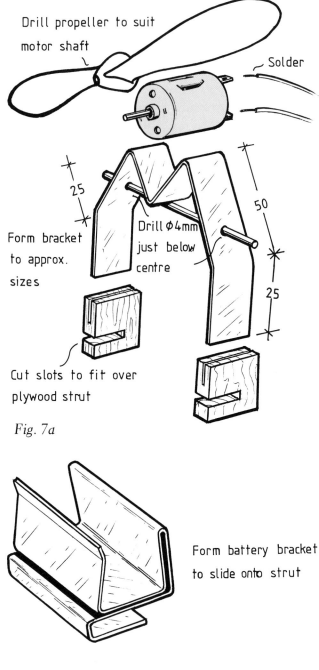

Drill propeller to suit
motor shaft

Solder

25

Form bracket
to approx.
sizes

Drill φ4mm
just below
centre

50

25

Cut slots to fit over
plywood strut

Fig. 7a

Things to do and to find out

1 Redesign your own mounting bracket.

2 How can you avoid having loose 'slots' on
your bracket-to-slide mounts?

3 Which terminal on the motor is positive?
How will you find out to ensure forward
propulsion on your boat?

4 Do you need to protect your motor from the
water? How can you do this?

5 Fit a rudder to the boat which can be
adjusted so that the boat will go in circles of
chosen diameters.

6 Draw boxes and show the input-to-output
changes that take place when the boat is
sailing under motor power.

7 Sketch the circuit diagram for your power
unit.

8 Design a colour scheme for your boat and
decorate it.

9 What effect does changing the propeller size
have on the performance of your boat?

Form battery bracket
to slide onto strut

Fig. 7b

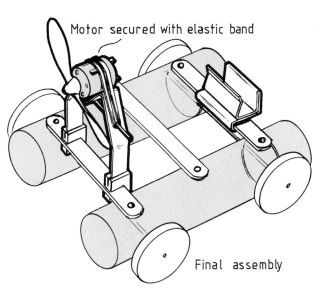

Motor secured with elastic band

Final assembly

Fig. 7c

FLIGHT

Introduction

Humans have always been fascinated by the flight of birds. They have tried to copy birds over the years.

History has shown that many 'designers' have perished when testing their ideas, because their theories were wrong or the methods and materials used in building their gliders and aeroplanes were not suitable (Fig. 1).

Fig. 1

Flight is an area when the technologist is all-important. He or she must understand the theory of flight, the effects of controls added to the aircraft and be able to select the correct materials in terms of their weight and strength. In a limited way this is what you will be attempting to do in this section. Some of the necessary theory was covered in section 2 on propellers. Refresh your memory and read it again.

You have no doubt tried making paper gliders with some success. One problem with paper gliders in particular is that of unwanted creasing of the paper. This creates problems. There only has to be a slight distortion of this material and you may as well start again, as you cannot easily eliminate (remove) these faults. We are going to look at some materials that are a little more robust and will allow you to experiment without continually having to make a fresh glider.

How to make your basic glider

1. Discarded expanded polystyrene food trays or tiles are a cheap source of material from which to build a glider. Because it is light and yet quite strong (a property of polystyrene), expanded polystyrene is a very suitable choice.

2. Three examples are given in Figure 2. Note that the size of the tray will determine the glider's wing size.

3. You will need a sharp, thin cutting blade such as a modelling knife, or you can make desired slots by using a needle and piercing holes around the shape required.

4. Use a Biro pen top to make a hole for a Plasticine weight.

5. Three different tail sections are shown (Figs. 2a, b, c).

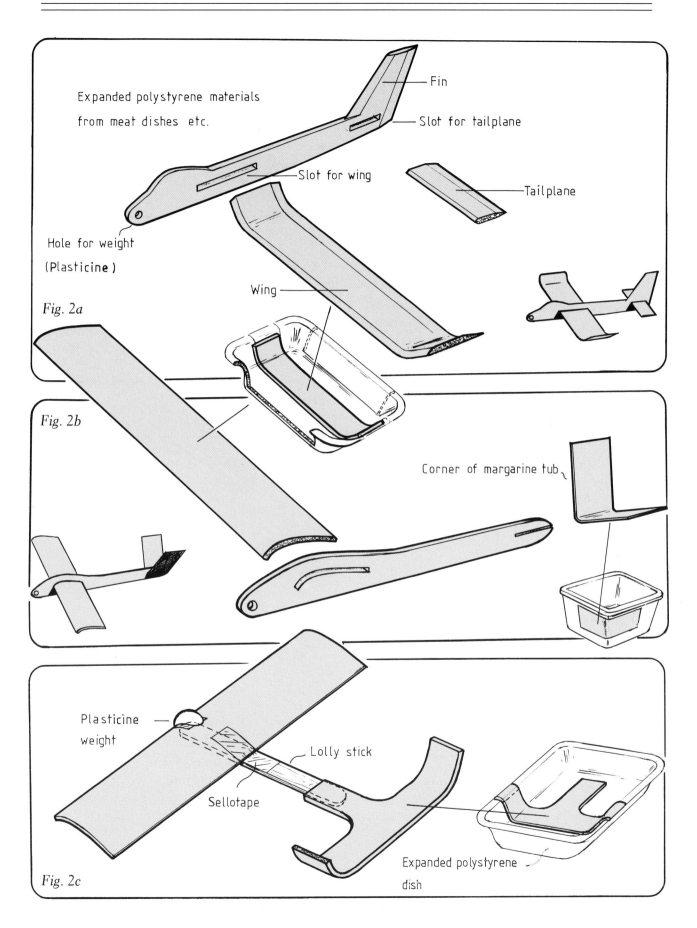

Expanded polystyrene materials from meat dishes etc.

Fin

Slot for tailplane

Slot for wing

Tailplane

Hole for weight

(Plasticine)

Wing

Fig. 2a

Fig. 2b

Corner of margarine tub

Plasticine weight

Lolly stick

Sellotape

Expanded polystyrene dish

Fig. 2c

Try these examples and experiment yourself to obtain results and, once you have made progress, move on to the next brief.

Brief 12.1

Design a glider to demonstrate the effects of controls.

A glider or aeroplane has three basic control surfaces: the elevators on the tailplane, ailerons on the ends of each wing and the rudder on the fin. Let us attach a control surface to these areas and see what happens.

An easy to build and successful design is the delta wing shape.

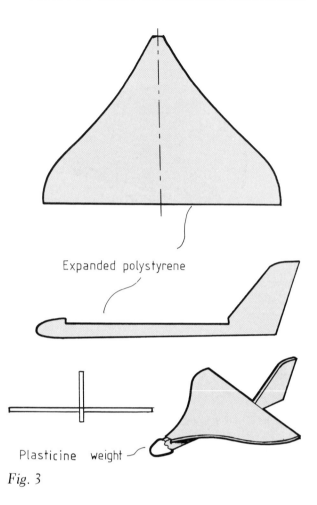

Expanded polystyrene

Plasticine weight

Fig. 3

How to make the delta glider (Fig. 3)

1 Cut the wing and fuselage shapes from a polystyrene food tray.

2 Glue two shapes together using one of the recommended 'stick' glues for polystyrene.

3 Add weight so that when you launch the glider it glides in the way shown.

4 The method of launching is very important: a smooth, gentle arm movement is necessary. The glider needs to travel in a straight line in a very slight downward direction (Fig. 4).

5 Cut five pieces of paper for use as control surfaces of a size to suit your glider (approx. 25 mm × 10 mm).

6 Sellotape the controls to the delta glider (Fig. 5).

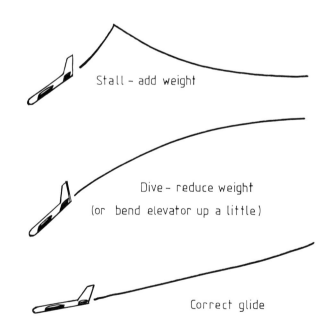

Stall – add weight

Dive – reduce weight
(or bend elevator up a little)

Correct glide

Fig. 4

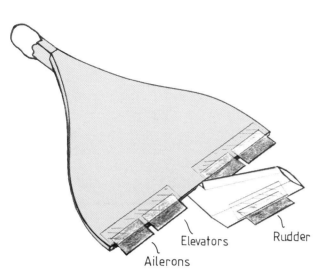

Elevators   Rudder

Ailerons

Fig. 5

9 Set the rudder right, launch the glider and observe what happens (Fig. 6f).

10 Set the rudder left, launch the glider and observe. Explain the reasons for the changes that you see (Fig. 6g).

The need for close observation and recording is important. We want to know what happens *as soon as* we launch. Further changes occur, but it is both difficult to explain them in theory and observe in practice. We will restrict our observations to the first effects only. Move on to the next brief.

Things to do and to find out

1 Check that all control surfaces are neutral (that they are in line with the wing or fin and do not protrude into the airflow) (Fig. 6a).

2 Launch the glider and check for a straight glide.

3 Set the elevators to an up position and launch the glider (Fig. 6b). Explain what happens.

4 Set the elevators to the down position and launch the glider (Fig. 6c). Explain what happens.

5 Return the elevator to the neutral position.

6 Set the port (left) aileron to up and the starboard (right) aileron to down (Fig. 6d). Launch the glider and observe the results.

7 Reverse the instructions given in step 6 (Fig. 6e). Explain what happens.

8 Set the ailerons to neutral, launch the glider and *check* for the straight glide.

Brief 12.2

Design a catapult glider (Photo 1).

You will have found out from your previous brief that the elevators make the nose of the glider go up or down (pitch). The ailerons cause the glider to bank left or right (roll) and the rudder makes the glider crab sideways (yaw).

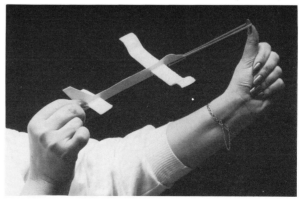

Photo 1

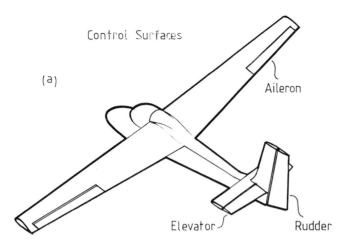

Control Surfaces

(a)

Aileron

Elevator

Rudder

Now that you have learnt the basic theory of flight, let us use an elastic band to provide the energy to launch our glider. Only a slight modification (change) of design is necessary, although you may find a change of materials will help improve performance.

How to convert to a catapult system (Fig. 7)

Three ideas are shown in Figure 7a, b, c.

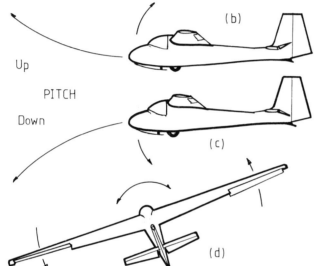

Up

PITCH

Down

(b)

(c)

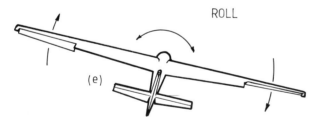

ROLL

(d)

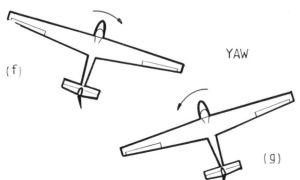

YAW

(e)

(f)

(g)

Fig. 6

Things to do and to find out

1 List the energy changes that take place when you launch your glider (Fig. 7d).

2 How does the flight of the catapult glider differ from the flight of the hand-launched one?

3 What happens when (a) a weak (b) a strong elastic band is used?

4 Try controlling the flight of the glider using the method shown in brief 12.1.

5 Change the materials used in the example to those of your own choice.

6 How important is the balance of the glider? Design a way of checking the balance (centre of gravity) before launching. One way is shown in Figure 8. Push a needle into the end of each wing about one-third from the front of the wing. Add weights until the glider remains level (balances) without any tendency to pitch up or down.

7 What is the furthest distance your catapult glider will fly? List the changes or modifications you have made to its design to achieve this.

8 Try launching the glider *into* wind and then *with* the wind. Are there any differences in performance? If so, what are they?

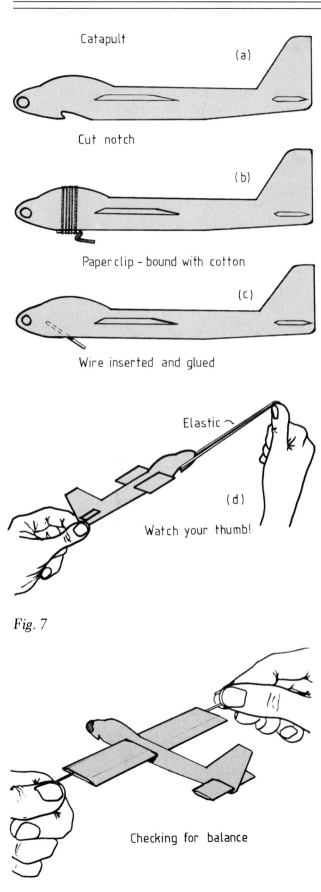

Catapult
(a)

Cut notch
(b)

Paperclip – bound with cotton
(c)

Wire inserted and glued

Elastic
(d)

Watch your thumb!

Fig. 7

Checking for balance

Fig. 8

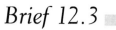

Brief 12.3

Design a wind-producing unit to help test your glider or aeroplane (Photo 2).

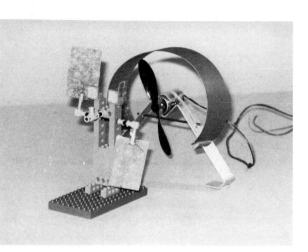

Photo 2

Aeroplanes and vehicles cannot be tested easily outside, where they would be using natural movements of air. There are too many external (outside) influences that effect the airflow, i.e. rain, strong winds and turbulence, buildings, trees and contour of the ground. To overcome these factors a 'testing unit' or 'test house' is often built so that the design of the aeroplane, engine or smaller model can be checked for performance in controlled conditions.

One way in school of producing controlled movements of air is to use the 'blowing' end of a vacuum cleaner, but one vacuum cleaner is not enough for a whole class and it is costly to buy others. Making your own is one way of solving this problem.

How to make your own wind-producing unit

Chapter 11 on Boats shows an idea that, with modifications, can be used as a wind-producer.

Things to do and to find out

1 The unit shown in Chapter 11, Figure 7 is unstable (falls over easily) when the motor is switched on. Sketch ways of supporting the unit to stop it falling over.

2 How should the propeller be fitted to the motor shaft to obtain wind-producing results? Why?

3 What effect does a larger or three-bladed propeller have?

4 Use a Windcatcher made from Lego or other construction kit and test the unit.

5 Test for the wind energy produced by widening the gap between the unit and Windcatcher. Try to explain the effect.

6 *Now* use the test unit with your glider.

7 What happens when you reverse the electrical connections to the motor?

Brief 12.4

Design a motorised glider (an aeroplane) with a magnetic release system (Photo 3).

Aeroplanes are used in air–sea rescue to locate people in difficulties. They drop inflatable rafts or markers as close to survivors as possible. Should they miss their target the survivors may not have the energy to swim a great distance to the rafts.

You can test your target release skills for accuracy and timing in this brief and test yourself against friends.

How to make your magnetic release aeroplane (Fig. 9)

1 Cut a strip of wood to a size of 600 × 15 × 10 mm.

2 Mark out and drill two holes (Fig. 9a).

3 Make a pivot bracket from thin-gauge aluminium to the approximate sizes shown (Fig. 9b).

4 Drill two holes (to suit screw sizes) and make a centre punch mark *inside* the centre of the bracket (Fig. 9c).

5 File a slight groove in the top surface of the wood to suit the motor (Fig. 9d).

6 Make a mounting for the motor (Fig. 9e).

7 Drill two holes to suit the screws (Fig. 9e).

8 Make a body for the magnet from a piece of dowel, nylon or other insulating material (Fig. 9f).

9 Wrap three layers of insulation neatly around the barrel of the body (Fig. 9g).

10 Turn an aluminium slip-ring on the lathe to ∅ 12 × 20. Face ends, centre drill and drill hole through ∅ 6. Press a ∅ 6 wood dowel into the drilled hole. Redrill the hole through the dowel with a ∅ 3 drill. Saw a slight groove near one end of ring (Fig. 9h).

11 Make a pivot from ∅ 3 rod and cut it to approximately 150 mm length. Attach the slip-ring to the rod, to suit the paper-clip contact (Fig. 9h).

12 Use a nail as the soft iron core of the magnet. Cut it to size and push it into a ∅ 3.0 hole on the end of the wooden rail (Fig. 9g).

13 Screw the bracket and motor into position close to or above the magnet (Fig. 9i).

Photo 3

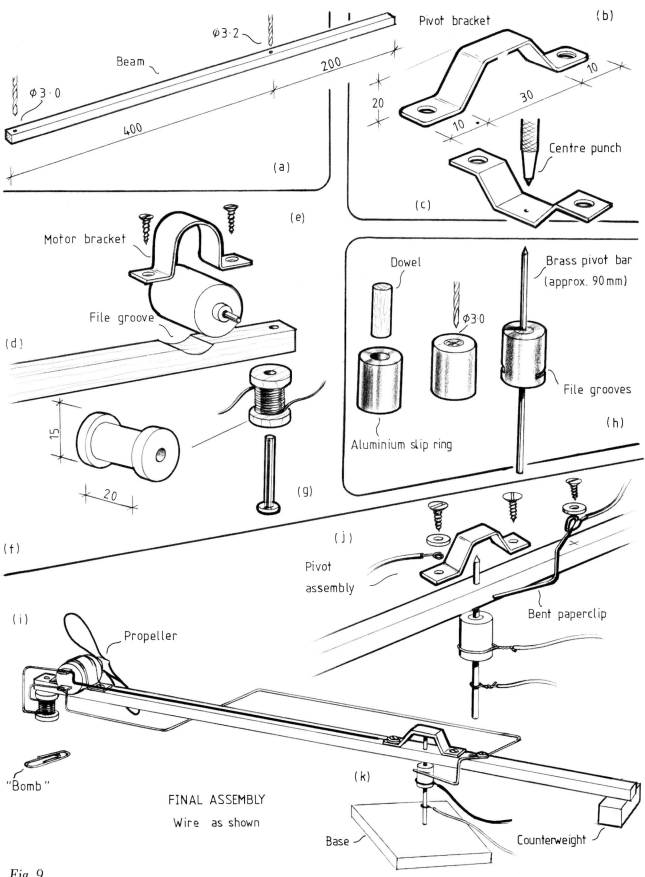

φ3·2
Beam
200
φ3·0
400
(a)

Pivot bracket (b)
10
20
30
10
Centre punch
(c)

Motor bracket (e)
File groove
(d)

Dowel
Brass pivot bar (approx. 90mm)
φ3·0
File grooves
Aluminium slip ring
(h)

15
20
(g)

(f)

Pivot assembly (j)
Bent paperclip

(i)
Propeller

"Bomb"
FINAL ASSEMBLY
Wire as shown
(k)
Base
Counterweight

Fig. 9

14 Screw the pivot bracket into position above the centre hole, ensuring the pivot end lines up with the centre punch mark (Fig. 9j).

15 Shape the paper clip and mount it close to the pivot bracket.

16 Cut wires to suit distances between motor and brackets.

17 Strip ends of all wires.

18 Solder wires into position (for soldering see brief 10.5).

A suitable block of metal or wood with a hole drilled in the centre is required, into which the pivot end is placed. Finally the motor and propeller will require a counterbalance on the other end of the rail (Fig. 9k).

Things to do and to find out

1 When making the magnet, check its magnetism with the nail in position – before assembling the rail. Does a paper clip 'stick' to it?

2 Remove the nail – does the magnet still work? Explain any differences and give reasons for them.

3 What is the purpose of the slip ring?

4 Try batteries of different voltages from 1½ volts upwards.

NOTE

Do not exceed the maximum recommended voltage for your motor! Why not?

5 Can friction in the unit be reduced in any way?

6 As the unit rotates, release the paper clip so that it drops on the target. How is this achieved?

7 Problems of magnetism occur in using this unit – what are they? How can you overcome them? (Look at step 10 below for hints.)

8 Is a rheostat required in the circuit? Why?

9 Electrical contact may be a problem using the slip ring. How can this be improved?

10 Use a two-way switch to help you release the paper clip.

11 What are the energy inputs and outputs of the unit?

12 Research other ways of improving the design.

Brief 12.5

Use the previous unit and modify (change) it to test wind resistance.

Brief 12.6

Design an electrically powered unit to help demonstrate control functions of an aeroplane (Photo 4).

Photo 4

As you progress through these briefs, the accuracy required and the level of difficulty will increase. Design and testing requires patience by the technologist in solving problems, eliminating inefficiencies and improving on results in any way possible. Record results to ensure that such tests are not repeated unnecessarily. This should be done with this problem.

The idea shown is *very* sensitive to changes. Because of the experience you now have, less information is given on how to make this unit.

Things to do and to find out

1 Make a pivot and test the plane as shown in Figures 10 and 11.

2 Adjust the controls to neutral and balance the Glidaplane.

3 Adjust the elevator to make the nose pitch up and switch on the unit. What has happened to the Glidaplane's attitude?

4 Repeat step 3 with the elevator set to produce a nose-down attitude.

Brief 12.7

Design a model aeroplane powered by an elastic band.

Use the information given in these briefs and look at the method of attaching a propeller and band to the examples in Brief 11.3.

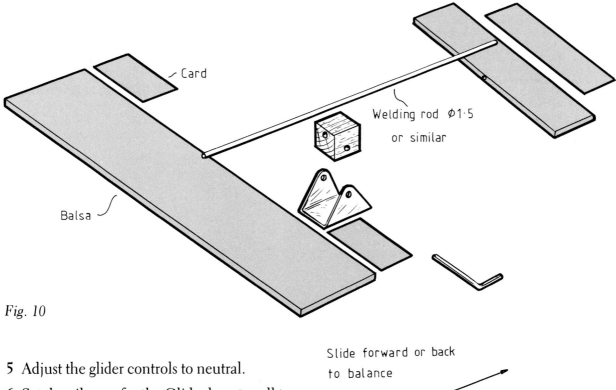

Fig. 10

5 Adjust the glider controls to neutral.

6 Set the ailerons for the Glidaplane to roll to the right.

7 Repeat paragraph 6 for the Glidaplane to roll to the left.

8 Explain the changes.

9 In a glider or aeroplane with the controls set as in our model the aircraft would continue to roll. Why does our model not do this?

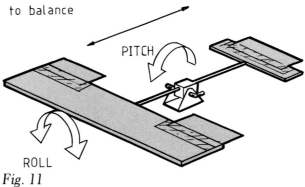

Fig. 11

LEVERS AND LINKAGES

Introduction

Designing moving (mechanical) figures may appear to be difficult. Trace the one shown in Figure 1, cut it out, colour and assemble it. You will find it absorbing to build and find out what is meant by levers and pivots. You can then design your own Moveapart quite easily.

The Moveapart face is made from card, Sellotape and four paper fasteners. Assembly is straightforward and, as you complete each stage, more mechanical movements are added. When it is finished you will have what appears to be a complicated figure – only you know that it isn't! (Photo 1).

Photo 1

How to make your mechanical face

1 Place a thin sheet of white paper over the parts shown, as in Figure 1.

2 Trace around the shapes and cut them out.

3 Glue the shapes onto a cereal box card and cut them out.

4 Use a small-hole paper punch or a sharp pencil to make holes A and B in the face and ears (Figs 1a and b).

5 Use a modelling knife and cut slits for the mouth and eye parts.

6 Make the two sliders for the face, one for the hat and one for the tie as shown in Figure 1c. Sellotape them into place (Figs 1d and e).

7 Slide the eye and mouth parts (Figs 1f and g) into place on the lever (Fig. 1h).

8 Pass the lever through the sliders on the head (Fig. 1a).

9 Pass the fasteners through the A holes of the head and ears.

10 Set the ears vertically, insert an elastic band (or cotton) between the B holes and staple (or glue) the ends to the card. Sellotape or staple the middle of the band to position 1 on the lever.

11 Slide the hat (Fig. 1e) and tie (Fig. 1i) on to the ends of the lever.

12 Adjust the parts until all the mechanisms function (work) properly. Sellotape where necessary to keep them in the correct position.

13 Colour your Moveapart face.

Things to do and to find out

1 Explain the difference between a fixed pivot, a moving pivot and a slider. What is their purpose?

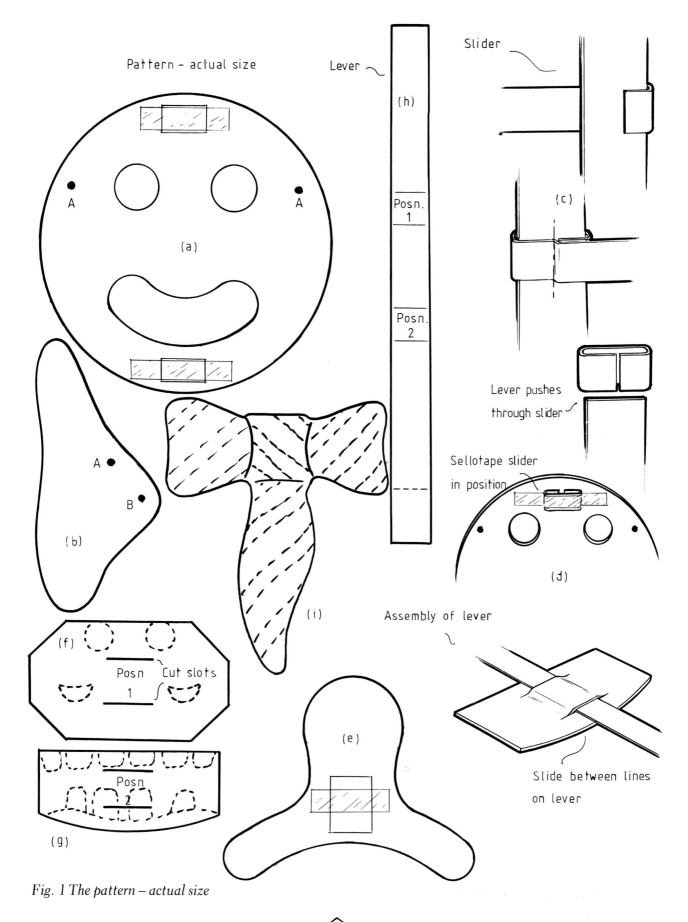

Pattern – actual size

Lever

(h)

Posn.
1

Posn.
2

Slider

(c)

Lever pushes
through slider

Sellotape slider
in position

(d)

A   A

(a)

A
B

(b)

(i)

(f)

Posn   Cut slots
1

Posn
2

(g)

(e)

Assembly of lever

Slide between lines
on lever

Fig. 1 The pattern – actual size

2 What is the effect in mechanical movement if the pivot holes are (a) closer together, (b) further apart?

3 Think of other ways to hold the Moveapart together.

4 Try adding extras to improve its features, i.e. wool for hair, balloon for the tongue, a ping-pong ball nose etc.

Brief 13.1

Design and make your own Moveapart figure from stronger materials.

A cardboard moveapart is shown in Photo 2. Using this to prove that your ideas will work is quick and easy. The levers are strips of plywood, holes are drilled slightly larger where necessary to allow movement and slightly less in diameter in the body so a push fit of the rivet is obtained.

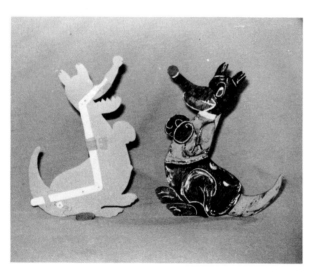

Photo 2

Things to do and to find out

1 Why do we use card to prove our design in the early stages?

2 Use Meccano to help solve your problems of leverage or linkage.

3 Make a Moveapart 'picture' by attaching your idea to a board and framing it.

4 Try including elastic bands and other ideas to obtain a 'return' on your mechanism.

Brief 13.2

Design a crank-operated Moveapart (Photo 3).

Photo 3

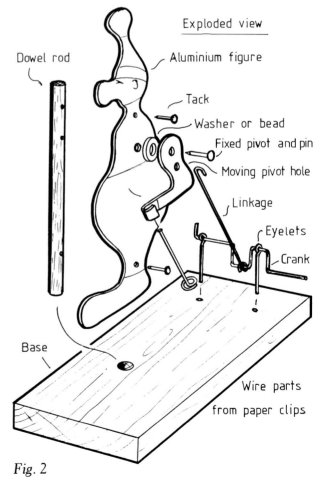

Exploded view

Dowel rod

Aluminium figure

Tack

Washer or bead

Fixed pivot and pin

Moving pivot hole

Linkage

Eyelets

Crank

Base

Wire parts from paper clips

Fig. 2

You may have used the mechanism of a crank in previous briefs. Remember: the crank produces a rotary (round) movement and you convert (change) this into linear (straight) movement. The crank is 'old' technology and yet is still very necessary today. Cranks have been used to help raise water from wells for hundreds of years, and you use a crank every time you ride your bicycle!

How to make a cranked Moveapart (Fig. 2)

1 Design a shape for the figure of your Moveapart.

2 Make it simple by only having one moving limb.

3 Cut off a piece of dowel support rod and fit it to a wood base.

4 Line up the basic figure with the rod and mark out holes for the pivots.

5 Make an arm for your figure.

6 Drill two holes in the arm (your earlier brief will give you an idea where to drill the holes).

7 Attach the figure to the support with tacks.

8 Bend paper clips to make the crank, linkage to arm, eyelets and ski stick.

9 Drill holes in the base for the eyelets.

10 Paint your figure.

Things to do and to find out

1 The arm linkage has to be free to move – small beads instead of washers can be used to keep the arm loose and in place.

2 Making the crank is difficult – a long-nosed pair of pliers and patience will help you here!

3 Try to design the movement of the arm to copy that of a skier. Experiment with hole

positions and the size of the crank to achieve good results.

4 Think of a better way of fixing the crank and eyelets in place. Perhaps a U-shaped bracket would be useful?

Remember: it's more fun to solve problems yourself – not all the answers are given.

Brief 13.3

Design a mechanical arm that can be operated with one hand only (Photo 4).

A 'handgrab' is a way of simulating (copying) nature. It is a mechanical device that will pick things up and put them down in the same way that we do with our arms and hands. Many 'grabs' have been designed as aids to the handicapped, the aged, the infirm and also in industry with the new technology of automated machinery and robotically-built motor cars. Your handgrab could be modified to retrieve lost balls in trees or those apples that cannot be reached!

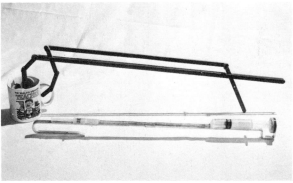

Photo 4

Two examples are shown. Each of them can be redesigned in many ways.

How to make your Moveapart handgrab

Example 1 (Fig. 3)

1 Decide on the object you wish to pick up or retrieve. How does this affect the handgrab?

2 The example shown can be made from strips of thin timber.

3 Try making a model using Meccano (Photo 5).

4 The example shows an elastic band being used to close the moving pivot jaw. Make a handgrab with the band opening a jaw.

5 What sort of force is applied to the string to allow you to open the jaws in Figure 3?

6 Make the longest handgrab you can.

7 Sketch other ideas for assembly of the handgrab parts.

8 What decides the size of the handle for the grab?

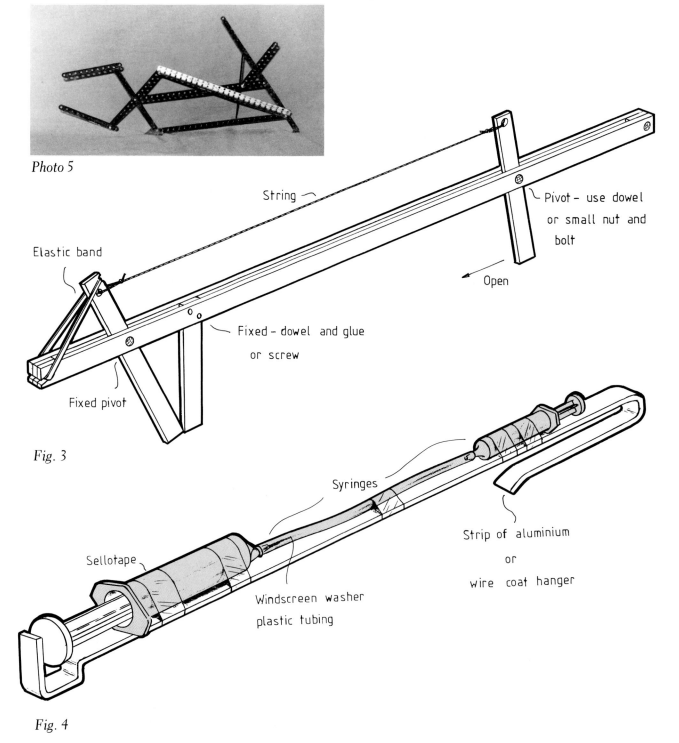

Photo 5

Fig. 3

Fig. 4

9 Use other materials and make your own grab.

10 The jaws of the handgrab can be made to look like arms or legs. Design such a feature into yours.

Example 2 (Fig. 4 and Photo 5)

1 Obtain two syringes of different sizes if possible and some car windscreen washer plastic tubing.

2 Attach the tubing to the ends of each syringe. Fill the syringes with water.

3 If the syringes are of different sizes, try pushing one against the other. Compare the force used in each case and the distance travelled by each piston. Do you come to any conclusions?

4 Bend a thin piece of aluminium strip (or you can even use a coat hanger) to the shape of that in the diagram.

5 Attach the syringes to the handgrab frame, using clips or Sellotape. Pick up the heaviest object you can.

6 Reverse the syringes and again pick up the heaviest article you can. What are the differences between the two? Explain the changes.

7 Which design is better? Compare their advantages and disadvantages.

8 Remove the water from the syringes and try the handgrab. What changes have now occurred?

9 Which is the better method, air or water?

10 List the energy changes that take place when you are using the handgrab.

11 Where else can you imagine syringes being used to demonstrate their advantages?

Brief 13.4

Design a cam-acting Moveapart (Photo 6).

Photo 6

A crank, as you have seen, changes rotary motion into linear. The cam acts in a similar way. We know that a wheel usually has the axle in its centre and the wheel will then turn concentrically (evenly). Our cam-acting mechanism is obtained by moving the axle away from its centre position. The wheel will now turn eccentrically (unevenly). The Moveapart will 'hop' along the surface on which it runs.

How to make a cam-acting Moveapart (Fig. 5)

1 A clear plastic container such as the top half of a bottle is a good choice, because you can see what is happening.

2 Drill holes to suit the axle size and the peg in the bottle neck (Fig. 5a).

3 Cut and shape two wheels from plastic (see the Introduction to section 3).

4 Drill two holes in each wheel for the axle and drive pin approximately 10 mm apart (Fig. 5b).

5 Obtain four beads and drill holes in them to suit the axle for a tight fit (Fig. 5c).

6 Measure the width of the bottle, the diameter of the four beads, the thickness of the two wheels and include an allowance for bending the ends of the axle. Cut the axle to length.

7 Bend one end of the axle to a 15 mm length. Slide on a bead, a wheel and a second bead. Push the axle through the

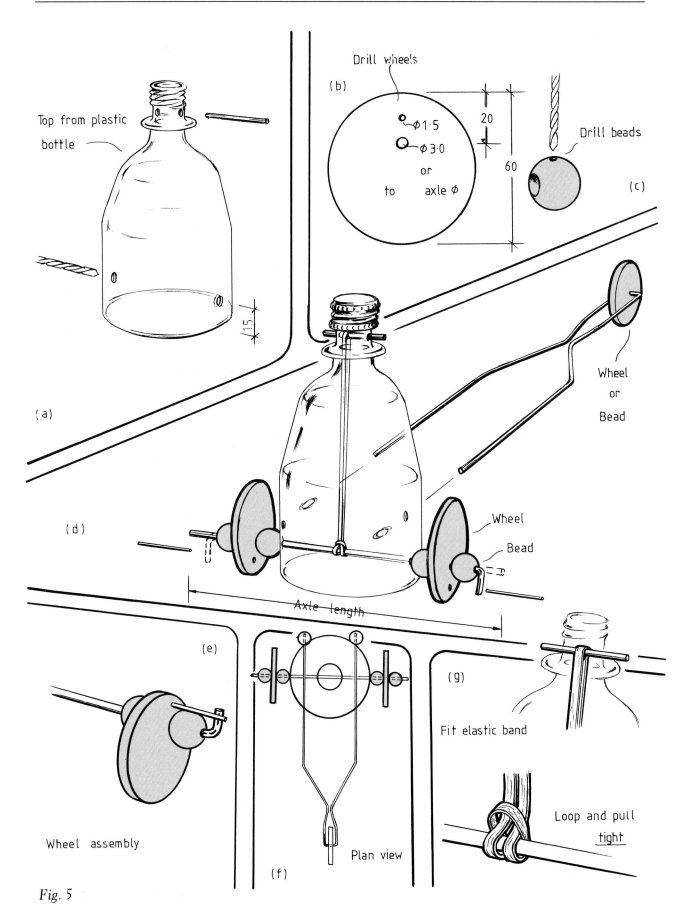

Top from plastic bottle

(a)

(b) Drill wheels

φ 1·5
φ 3·0
or
to   axle φ

20
60

Drill beads

(c)

Wheel or Bead

(d)

Wheel
Bead

Axle length

(e)
Wheel assembly

(f)
Plan view

(g)
Fit elastic band

Loop and pull **tight**

Fig. 5

bottle, slide on a third bead, the second wheel and the last bead into position (Fig. 5d).

8 Because the bottle is flexible, you can now bend the other end of the axle, but first push the parts along the axle to reduce any surplus axle length and yet still allow the wheels to rotate freely. Mark this position. You can now squash the bottle slightly; push the parts along the axle so that you can bend the end of the axle on the marked line. Keep this bend in line with the first.

9 Push the drive pin in the Ø 1.5 mm hole of the wheel. Ensure the pin is long enough to make contact with the bend in the axle (Fig. 5e).

10 Design and attach a tail to the cam Moveapart (Figs 5d and f).

11 Loop an elastic band around the axle and then to the pin in the top of the bottle (Fig. 5g).

12 Wind the wheels to energise the band.

13 Place the Moveapart on floor and see it hop!

Photo 7

Things to do and to find out

1 Before attaching the tail, try pushing the Moveapart along the floor and see what happens.

2 Energise the Moveapart and repeat step 1 above.

3 What is the purpose of the tail?

4 The tail does not *need* a bead fitted to it, but it works better with one. Explain why this is so.

5 Attach strong thick elastic bands and then thin long ones to your Moveapart. Explain the effect of each. Which is the better type to use?

6 Use other materials for the body. An example is shown in Photo 7 using aluminium for the body. What advantages or disadvantages does this have over the plastic bottle?

7 List the energy changes that take place using the cam-acting Moveapart.

8 Design more features into your Moveapart.

Brief 13.5

Design a noise-producing toy vehicle (Photo 8).

Photo 8

You have already made a crank-operated vehicle in brief 3.1. This brief takes the mechanisms idea a little further; you can now use the knowledge you acquired earlier by modifying your vehicle to create further movement with noise as well. One idea using a plastic container is shown in Figure 6.

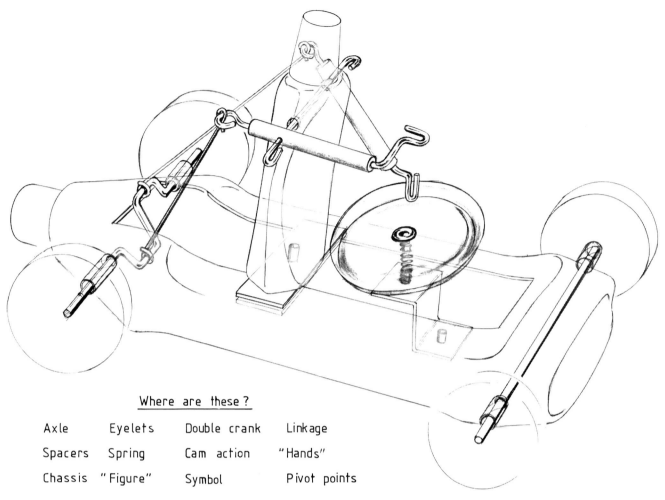

Where are these?

Axle	Eyelets	Double crank	Linkage
Spacers	Spring	Cam action	"Hands"
Chassis	"Figure"	Symbol	Pivot points

Fig. 6

How to make your noisy mechanism

1 Obtain a flat plastic container and cut a slot in one of the flat sides.

2 Make a straight and a cranked axle (Fig. 6).

3 Drill holes for your axles into the body.

4 Make four wheels and assemble them to the axles and vehicle.

5 Use a second container as a figure to be fixed to your vehicle body.

6 Drill holes in the figure container, to which will be fitted the 'arm' axle.

7 Make two arms from a dowel and drill a hole through the dowel and in each end.

8 Make two eyelets and two hands from coathanger wire.

9 Remove the base of an aluminium can.

10 Fix a spring to the can base, with a small nut and bolt.

11 Attach the other end of the spring to the inside of the vehicle body.

12 Connect thin wire linkages from the crank to the eyelets of the arms.

TEST YOUR IDEAS

Brief 14.1: Spring balance tester

Design a spring balance to be used in your Testaband project (Photo 1).

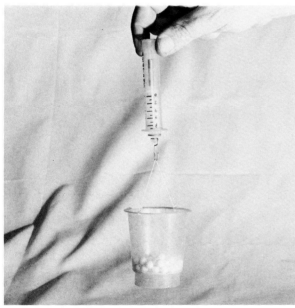

Photo 1

Once you have designed this balance it can of course be used in other experiments. One way of making such a balance is shown in Figure 1. You will need a tension (pull) spring; these can be obtained from scrap washing machines or similar devices. The only other part you require is a syringe.

How to make your tension spring balance

1 Remove the nozzle from the outer cylinder (Fig. 1a).

2 Check the length of your tension spring.

3 Cut the inside plunger into separate lengths to suit your spring (Fig. 1b).

4 Drill a small hole in each plunger to hook the springs onto (Fig. 1c).

5 Shape a paper clip to fit onto the bottom of the plunger to be used as a hook for your weights etc. (Fig. 1d).

6 Mark out a scale for your spring balance, choosing a suitable place to start from a zero line (Fig. 1e).

Things to do and to find out

1 How will you gauge the length of your plungers?

2 How are you going to mark the scale accurately?

3 Which is better for your balance: a short fat compression spring or a long thin one?

4 Make your own tension spring tester.

5 Why is an elastic band unsuitable for replacing the spring?

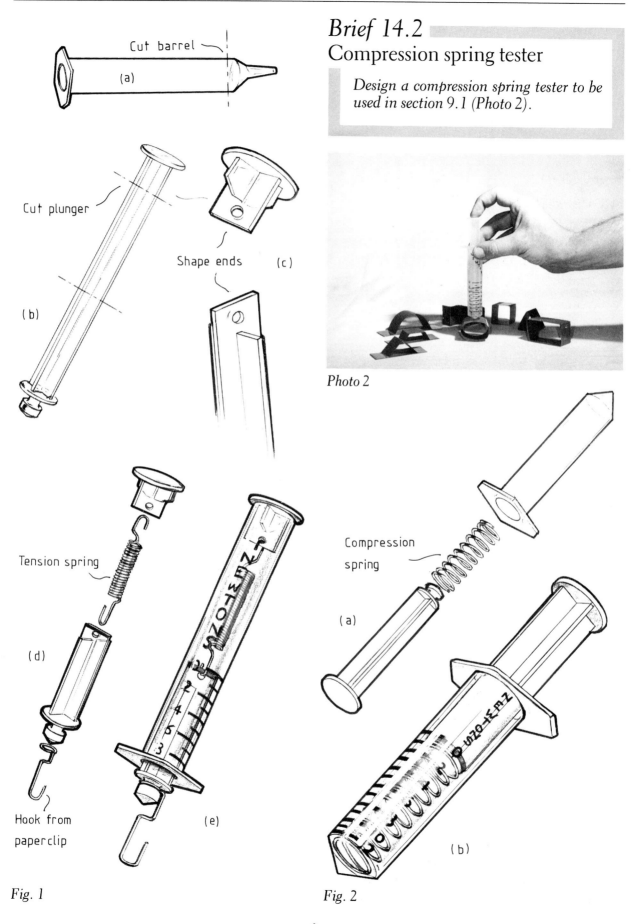

Cut barrel

(a)

Cut plunger

Shape ends (c)

(b)

Tension spring

(d)

Hook from
paperclip

(e)

Fig. 1

Brief 14.2
Compression spring tester

Design a compression spring tester to be used in section 9.1 (Photo 2).

Photo 2

Compression
spring

(a)

(b)

Fig. 2

Sometimes it may be necessary to measure the compression (push) loads that you may apply. Now let us make a device to do just that. We can still use the syringe with modifications.

How to make your compression spring tester (Fig. 2)

1 Remove the nozzle from the outer tube.

2 Attach a suitable compression spring to the end of the plunger (Fig. 2a).

3 Mark a scale on your spring balance (Fig. 2b).

Things to do and to find out

1 When using your Brainstormer in section 9.1, is a weak or strong compression spring necessary? Explain your choice.

2 How will you measure and mark the scale accurately?

3 Try using this spring in section 6, the structures experiment, to check compression loads on the bridges.

4 Design your own compression spring tester.

Brief 14.3
Structures under test

> *Design a method of testing the strength of structures (Photo 3).*

Section 6 looked at the way structures such as bridges can be stiffened or strengthened. Here is one way of testing some of the shapes involved before they are used in construction.

Photo 3

Structures have to withstand static forces and dynamic forces. (Brainstormer 9.4). To test static loads we can progressively increase the weights applied to find out when the structure begins to break down. To check the dynamic load we can apply a moving force to the structure or have the structure move and apply it to a solid mount. Car structures, for example, are crashed against a solid wall. Vehicles are used in the following example.

How to make your structure tester

Example 1

1 Machine or cut and file two blocks of mild steel to a size of approximately 40 × 35 × 25 mm (Fig. 3).

2 Hacksaw two slots into each of the blocks.

3 Drill holes to take the axles.

4 Machine four wheels of Ø 25 × 10 mm from mild steel.

5 Drill holes in the wheels, to ensure a tight fit of the axle.

6 Assemble.

7 Make up structures from card as shown (Fig. 4).

8 Assemble the first structure to your blocks.

Things to do and to find out

1 Why is this unit made from mild steel?

2 How can you ensure your structures stay fixed into the slots of the blocks?

3 How can you record the force of the tester as it hits the wall?

4 Why is it necessary to weigh your tester?

5 What is the best slope to roll your vehicle down? How did you come to this conclusion?

6 Think of other ways of stiffening your structure.

7 What disadvantages are there with this design?

8 Check your structures for static loads by using your tester as in Figure 5. You can apply weights or use your compression spring tester you have made.

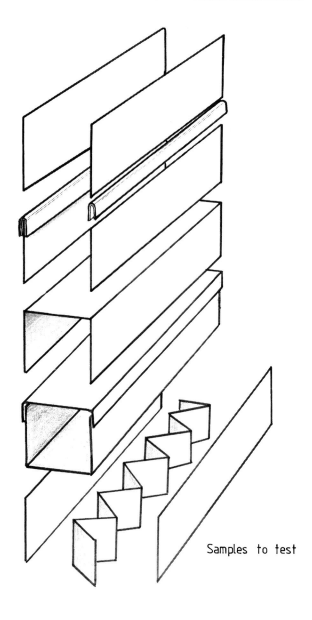

Samples to test

Fig. 4 Samples to test

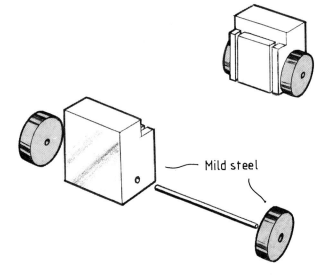

Mild steel

Fig. 3

Example 2 (Fig. 6 and Photo 4)
This is an easier-to-make tester.
1 Obtain two toy motor cars.
2 Drill a small hole into the roof of each car (to accept a small screw).

3 Make a wooden block as in Figure 6.

4 Screw the block to the cars.

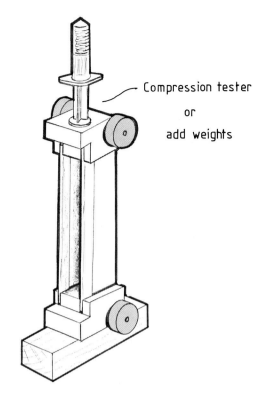

Compression tester

or

add weights

Fig. 5 Example 1

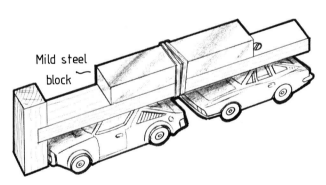

Mild steel block

Fig. 6 Example 2

Photo 4

Things to do and to find out

1 To increase the dynamic load, you can add weights to your tester. Secure them to the wooden block with an elastic band.

2 Repeat the experiments in Example 1 by rolling your tester into the structures.

3 Design your own way of testing these structures.

4 Replace structures you have designed by testing other shapes for strength such as egg box carton, match boxes etc.

Brief 14.4
Test a structure

Show how raising the centre of gravity of a vehicle makes it less stable.

When designing or experimenting, you can obtain unexpected results. The 'structure tester' did just that. Try this one and see for yourself. Use the Example 2 shown in the previous brief. It shows the need for you to keep an open mind when you look at designs to think how they may be used elsewhere. The idea came because the rear wheels of a motor car first fixed to the block were buckled and jammed occasionally. The vehicle was replaced, but an idea grew of simulating the braking of wheels on the vehicle to see the results.

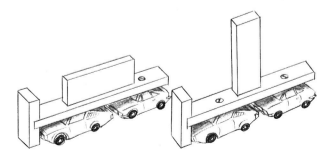

Fig. 7

Things to do and to find out

1 Without the weight on the vehicle, place it on a ramp and allow it to roll down a slope along a flat surface. Reverse it and see if any changes occur.

2 Sellotape the wheels on one of the cars to prevent them rotating.

3 Release the vehicle down the slope with the front wheels locked.

4 Release the vehicle down the slope with the rear wheels locked.

5 Add a weight to the wooden block and repeat steps 3 and 4 above.

6 Explain the results that you have seen. What conclusion can you reach?

7 Now attach a weight to your vehicle with a rubber band as shown in Figure 7. Roll your vehicle down the slope, with the rear wheels locked in each case.

8 What changes occurred? Does the vehicle now fulfil the brief given?

Brief 14.5
Electrical control

> Design a circuit to show how it can be used to control an electrically-powered vehicle.

We have experienced the basic circuit in some of the earlier briefs. Let us now take it a stage further and see how an electrical circuit can be used to control a vehicle. Once we can do this the theory can be used elsewhere quite easily. You can use a vehicle you have already made or design one from a construction kit (see Photo 5).

Photo 5

The electrical parts (components) we are going to use can be damaged quite easily by excessive heat through soldering. Our method of designing the circuit will allow you to construct it easily, reducing the soldering to a minimum.

We are going to use weak compression springs, which we 'bend' over. We then slide our components between the gap, clamping them into position (Fig. 8a). A suitable material for a circuit board can be almost any plastic container. Start with a flat piece initially, as the circuit will be easier to follow. The example shown (Photo 5) uses a toothpaste container. You will find that a hole can be either drilled into the container, or a sharp knitting needle can puncture it, making a hole to produce a tight fit on the spring – the plastic will grip the outside and your spring will stay in place (Fig. 8b).

How to make your control circuit

1 Copy the circuit of the spring positions only as in Figure 8c onto a piece of paper.

2 Glue the circuit onto your board, drill the holes and fit your springs.

3 Assemble the circuit (Fig. 8d).

Note the following important points:

Transistor: The base wire bends under the transistor and slides into the spring. Check the tag position.

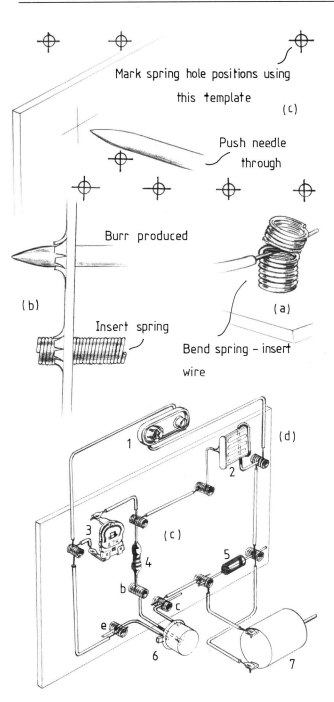

Mark spring hole positions using
this template
(c)

Push needle through

Burr produced

(b)

Insert spring

Bend spring – insert wire

(a)

(d)

1

2

3

(c)

4

5

b

c

e

6

7

1 : Battery connector

2 : LDR

3 : Pre-set Potentiometer (Variable Resistor)
    Wire to centre tag and any one of other two

4 : Resistor 2200 Ω

5 : Diode 1A – note position of dark ring

6 : Transistor BFY51 – note tag position

7 : Motor

Fig. 8

Diode: Assemble the diode with the ring on one end as shown in the assembly.

Pre-set potentiometer: When you are connecting the two wires, one must go to the centre tag. Solder two small wires to the pre-set for assembly to the board. The small centre screw can be turned to adjust the current in the circuit.

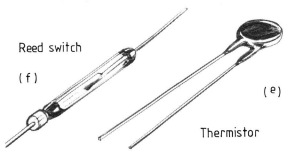

Reed switch
(f)

(e)

Thermistor

Fig. 9

Things to do and to find out

1 Fit your board to your vehicle.

2 Insert the LDR (light-dependent resistor) into your circuit. Shine a light onto it and explain what happens (Fig. 8d).

3 Insert the thermistor into your circuit (Fig. 9). Light a match and heat the wires to the thermistor. Explain the results.

4 Place a reed switch into your circuit (Fig. 9). Bring a magnet close to it. Explain what happens.

5 The components are hand-held to control the vehicle. Make them more permanent.

6 Remove the motor and replace it with a buzzer.

7 Modify your circuit to make a burglar alarm.

8 Use the circuit to make a rain alarm.

9 Design your own circuit on another board.

10 Explain the disadvantages you have found using the spring board.

11 The spring board allows you to design circuits by exchanging components. If you want to make a permanent circuit, then you will need to use a different type of board. Ask your teacher for assistance.

12 Sketch the circuit diagrams using the correct symbols.

The circuit uses the supply voltage from the computer user port and is used to switch lights on *only*. *Do not* connect a motor to this circuit. To control motors from a computer an interface *must* be used that converts a digital signal into an analogue signal and therefore stops damage being caused to your computer. You can, however, combine the previous brief and shine a light bulb from the computer on to the LDR of the vehicle circuit and obtain some very limited control.

Brief 14.6
Testacircuit

Design a circuit that can be used with a computer to show the traffic light sequence (Photo 6).

Photo 6

Computers are used to control many things in our everyday life. A typical use of computers is to control the traffic light sequences throughout our cities. Using the techniques of the previous brief you can now produce your own circuit and connect it to a BBC computer.

How to make your computer control circuit (Fig. 10)

1 Obtain a plastic container.

2 Using the circuit diagram shown, transfer the spring hole positions on to your container.

3 Drill the holes and fit the springs.

4 Obtain a 20-way cable mounting connector and length of ribbon cable. Clamp the cable connector at one end of your ribbon cable.

5 Split the ribbon cable as shown and tape the spare cable back. (You may want to use this in one of your own projects.)

6 Assemble the components to the container circuit.

7 Connect the cables from the ribbon to the circuit.

Note the following important points.

Transistor: Although a different transistor has been used the base, collector and emitter leads need to be connected as shown. Other types of transistor can be used if desired.

LED: Light-emitting diode – to be connected with the flat on the diode as shown.

You are now in a position to check your work. Plug the connection into the computer and the three LEDs should be on.

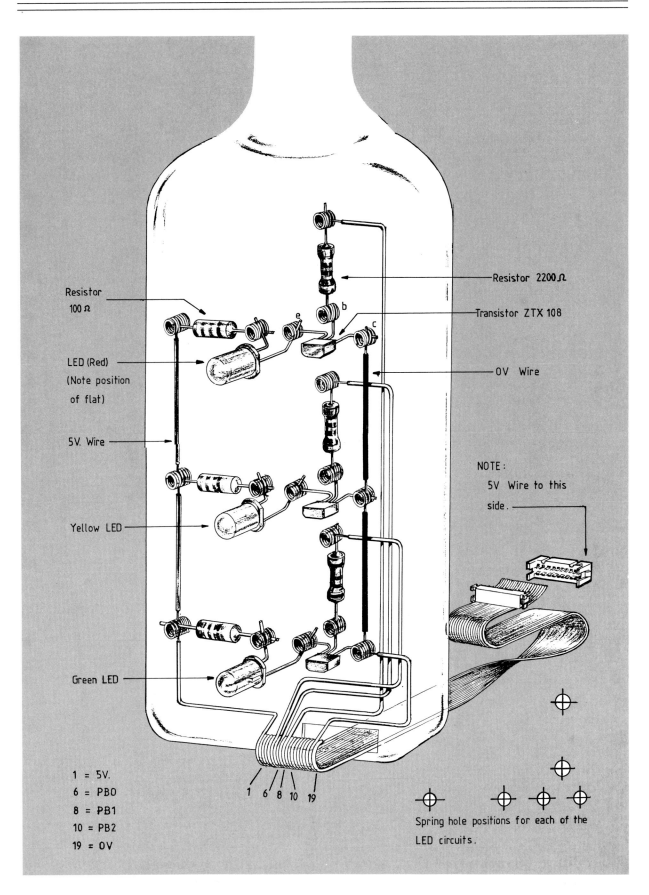

Resistor 2200 Ω

Resistor 100 Ω

Transistor ZTX 108

LED (Red)
(Note position
of flat)

0V Wire

5V. Wire

NOTE:
5V Wire to this
side.

Yellow LED

Green LED

1 = 5V.
6 = PB0
8 = PB1
10 = PB2
19 = 0V

Spring hole positions for each of the
LED circuits.

Fig. 10

A little theory

You obtain the traffic light sequence by switching on the correct pattern of LEDs when you type in the numbers on the keyboard. The numbers are stored in binary code in the user port's memory location. Each LED is connected to a bit in that memory and will switch on if the bit is 1 and off if the bit is 0.

The computer can control eight LEDs, although we are only using three of them. All eight are shown on so that you can see how binary code works.

	LED8	LED7	LED6	LED5	LED4	LED3	LED2	LED1
Binary	1	1	1	1	1	1	1	1
Denary	128	64	32	16	8	4	2	1

To switch on LED1 the following prefix is necessary ?&FE60 = 1
To switch on LED2 the following prefix is necessary ?&FE60 = 2
To switch on LED1 and 2 the following prefix is necessary ?&FE60 = 3
To switch on LED3 the following prefix is necessary ?&FE60 = 4
You can now see that to get number 5 in binary code we need to select LED1 and LED3 (1 + 4 = 5).

Traffic light sequence

The sequence is: red, red and amber, green, amber. This order is repeated and is called a *loop*. We program this loop into our computer.

Now you can start programming. Type in the following: 10 ?&FE62 = &FF:?&FE60 = 0 Press RETURN. This line may look complicated, but just use the figures at the start of each program. It is a routine line that sets the user port bits in the computer.

Type in the following:

110 ?&FE60 = 4 press RETURN, type RUN, press RETURN, check the LED.
120 ?&FE60 = 6 press RETURN, type RUN, press RETURN, check the LED.

130 ?&FE60 = 1 press RETURN, type RUN, press RETURN, check the LED.
140 ?&FE60 = 2 press RETURN, type RUN, press RETURN, check the LED.
160 ?&FE60 = 0 press RETURN, type RUN, press RETURN, check the LED.

You will have seen that the red LED is switched on by 4, red and amber by 6, the green by 1, amber by 2 and all the LEDs go out when 0 is used.

Type in the following: CLS press RETURN, LIST press RETURN. The program on the screen has now been 'tidied up'.

Type in the following: RUN and press RETURN. What did you observe? You will have seen the LEDs flash quickly through the sequence. We need a *delay* in our programme so that it can be seen working.

Type in the following:
115 FORX = 1TO2000:NEXTX   press RETURN.
125 FORX = 1TO2000:NEXTX   press RETURN.
135 FORX = 1TO2000:NEXTX   press RETURN.
145 FORX = 1TO2000:NEXTX   press RETURN.
160 FORX = 1TO2000:NEXTX   press RETURN.

Type RUN and press RETURN.

What changes have now occurred? You can see the traffic light sequence taking place. It only goes through the sequence once, and we want more!

Type in the following:

CLS press RETURN
LIST press RETURN
30 DEFPROCCOUNTNUMBEROFRUNS:LETC = C + 1:IFC>4THENGOTO160:ENDPROC   press RETURN.
150 PROCCOUNTNUMBEROFRUNS press RETURN.
Type RUN and press RETURN.

The sequence now repeats itself four times. If you want to repeat it more often change the 4 in line 30.

Type in the following: CLS press RETURN, LIST press RETURN.

Here is a line to improve the delay statement. Type in the following:

50 DEFPROCDELAY:FORX = 1TO2000:NEXTX:ENDPROC

Press RETURN, type RUN, press RETURN. It appears to make no difference to the operating sequence.

Type in the following:

115 PROCDELAY   press RETURN.
125 PROCDELAY   press RETURN.
135 PROCDELAY   press RETURN.
145 PROCDELAY   press RETURN.

Type CLS, press RETURN, type LIST, press RETURN, type RUN, press RETURN.

Can you see the change? The program begins to look neat and compact. One line such as line 50 can reduce unnecessary typing of repetitive statements. To increase or decrease the delay between the LEDs' flashing, change the 2000 figure in line 50.

You can now see the full program. If you have completed it without mistakes – well done!

The container circuit itself is a basic unit that can be used on all computers, but you will have to refer to the manual of your computer guide to check the electrical connections and method of programming. This brief is for BBC computers only.

Things to do and to find out

1 Read the line statements carefully and write down their meaning.

2 How would you keep the green on for longer periods? (Traffic lights on main roads would be programmed to remain on green longer than on side roads.)

3 Try programming the LEDs to count to 7 in binary code.

4 Use the previous brief and shine the LED from the computer onto its LDR. The vehicle moves! Think of other ways this idea could be used.

5 Draw a flow chart to show the sequence. Include the loops to the flow chart.

Program for traffic light sequence

```
10   ?&FE62 = &FF:?&FE60 = 0
20   LETC = 0
30   DEFPROCCOUNTNUMBEROFRUNS:
     LETC = C +
     1:IFC>3THENGOTO160:ENDPROC
50   DEFPROCDELAY:FORX =
     1TO2000:NEXTX:ENDPROC
110  ?&FE60 = 4
115  PROCDELAY
120  ?&FE60 = 6
125  PROCDELAY
130  ?&FE60 = 1
135  PROCDELAY
140  ?&FE60 = 2
145  PROCDELAY
150  PROCCOUNTNUMBEROFRUNS
155  GOTO110
160  ?&FE60 = 0
```

Brief 14.7
Testacircuit

Design and program a circuit to demonstrate binary counting using eight LEDs.

You have progressed a long way! Now extend the previous circuit of three LEDs to eight. Check your computer guide for correct wiring of the other LEDs. Get help from your teacher if you need it.

MAKING A REPORT

Brief 15.1

> Write a report on how you designed a rubber-powered vehicle to travel as quickly as possible over 20 metres (Photo 1).

Photo 1

An example of a vehicle is given. This brief is to show you how to write a report on its performance, the problems you found and how you solved them. Make this vehicle and see if your conclusions are the same. All problems encountered cannot be shown, as we do not have enough space to report on them.

This example is one to be made in school, as it is unlikely you have the facilities or materials at home. It is assumed you will have gone through Brief 10.1 thoroughly.

How to make your Report (Fig. 1)

1 Mark out the pattern (flat shape) of the body from aluminium (Fig. 1a).

2 Cut and file it to shape.

3 Drill four holes of Ø 1.5 mm and one of Ø 3.2 mm.

4 Bend (fold) the pattern to form the body (Fig. 1b).

5 Cut, file and joggle (bend) the attachment bracket – slide the aluminium plate into the joggle plate and squeeze it in a vice (Fig. 1c).

6 Rivet the bracket to the body (Fig. 1d).

7 Make two axle mounts (Fig. 1e).

8 Make one set of Perspex wheels and one of wood. Obtain two table-tennis balls.

9 Make a front wheel from Perspex or wood and obtain one bead.

10 Manufacture a plywood block to hold the propeller and keep the attachment bracket in position (Fig. 1f).

11 Cut axles of Ø 1.5mm and Ø 3.0 mm lengths to suit the axle mounts and wheels.

12 Cut a plastic washer to reduce friction between the propeller and wooden block.

13 Shape a paper clip to hold the propeller in place through the wooden block.

(Continued on page 124)

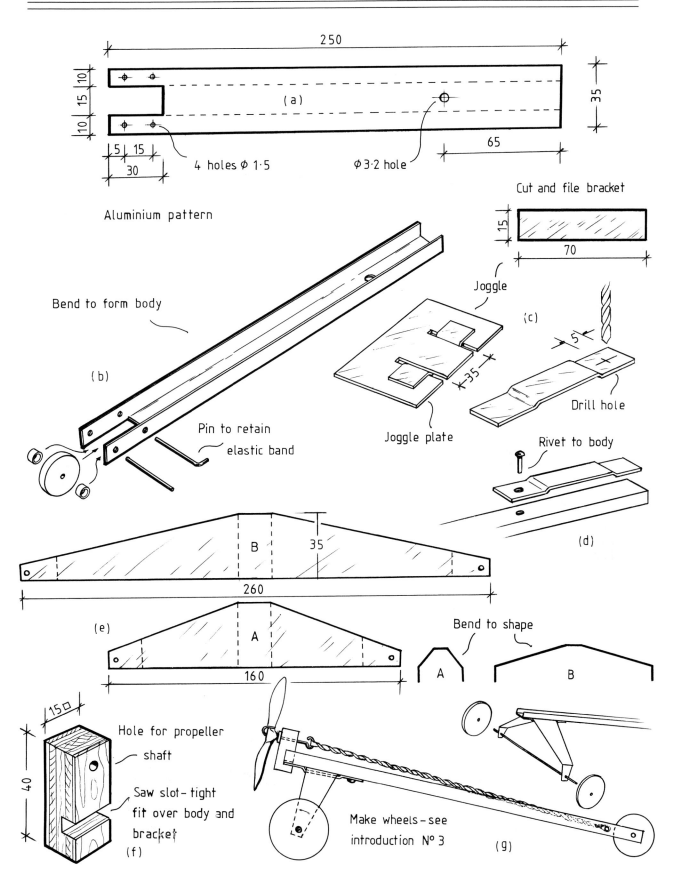

250

10 | 10
15
10

(a)

35

Ø 3·2 hole

65

5 | 15
30

4 holes Ø 1·5

Aluminium pattern

Cut and file bracket

15

70

Joggle

Bend to form body

(c)

35

5

Drill hole

(b)

Joggle plate

Pin to retain
elastic band

Rivet to body

(d)

B

35

Make wheels—see
introduction No 3

260

(e)

A

160

Bend to shape

A

B

15□

Hole for propeller
shaft

40

Saw slot—tight
fit over body and
bracket
(f)

(g)

Fig. 1

14 Obtain various elastic bands.

15 Cut a retaining pin for the elastic bands.

16 Obtain straws to be used as spacers.

17 Assemble the vehicle as shown in Figure 1g.

Report

(a) Materials and structure

A body of aluminium was decided upon, because of its lightness and ease of making. A bracket was used and a way was thought of to enable a quick change of axle mounts. Plastic was tried for the mounts, but it was found to be too heavy. The smallest diameter material and hole to suit was used for axles to reduce friction.

When axle mount A was used, the vehicle developed wheel spin and one side lifted off the ground. Various wheels were tried: plastic, wood and table-tennis balls. The introduction of the table-tennis balls appeared to reduce the lifting of one side – possibly because the axle had to be wider to be able to use them. A wider axle mount B was therefore used. This eliminated the lifting of one side of the vehicle. The lifting appeared to come from the twisting (torque) effect of the band as it unravelled. Wheel spin also appeared to be reducing with the increase in width – perhaps due to an increase in weight from the extra material.

(b) Mechanisms

The wheels were initially of all the same size, but the front of the vehicle rose. It also veered to the right as it went forward. Attempts were made to position the front single wheel to offset the veering, but this was found to be too difficult. The vehicle, however, did not veer to the right when released with a single wheel at the back. Larger wheels at the rear were added to stop the front coming off the ground and this appeared to work. The changing of the material of the small wheel had little or no effect on the vehicle's performance.

(c) Energy

Various elastic bands were used. Thick fat ones released energy quickly and the torque problem came back. Sixty turns of the band were the maximum that could be applied. Thin bands released energy slowly, the vehicle was slow to move off (accelerate) but did keep going over a longer distance. There were many turns still left on the band when the vehicle stopped. Over two hundred turns were used to get reasonable results from the vehicle. Medium bands in pairs were used and found to be best; one hundred to one hundred and fifty turns produced good results, the vehicle accelerated quickly, wheel spin occasionally occurred, but the vehicle covered the 10 metres quickly.

(d) Conclusions and development

With this vehicle the rear wheels have to be slightly larger than the front wheels to prevent the lift occurring. A wider rear axle is better than a narrow one, and table-tennis balls make good friction-free wheels. Pointing the vehicle slightly to the left at the start is better than trying to offset the front wheel to avoid the veer to the right. Thinner axles give better results than thicker ones, although the weaker axle allowed slight wheel wobble to take place.

 Things to do and to find out

1 Now make your own vehicle. Another example is shown in Photo 2.

Photo 2

2 Convert or modify the vehicle into the following:
(**a**) A land yacht.
(**b**) An electrically-powered vehicle.
(**c**) A balloon (air) powered vehicle.

NOTE

The main problem with balloon-power is the size of hole necessary to release air to start the vehicle rolling forward and to keep it moving before all the air is used up (Photo 3).

Photo 3

PROJECT

Introduction

'Build a roulette wheel' is included in this book to help those of you who have had only limited experience of making working models. Follow the instructions completely or, if you feel you can successfully make changes to the design, do so! When you have completed this example you will be able to tackle a whole range of working models with confidence.

Photo 1

Brief 16.1 Build a roulette wheel

> *The roulette wheel, when made, is only a start. You will have at your disposal a method of providing power to complete other projects using a motor, a battery and a rotating table – all that is needed is for you to design projects around these items (Photo 1).*

You will need the items shown in the table on the next page to complete this project.

How to make the roulette wheel

1 Cut and plane the base to size.

2 Cut and file items 13 (pivot support block) to size and deburr (Fig. 1a).

3 Cut and file item 14 to size and deburr.

4 Glue items 13 together. See note below.

5 Use wet and dry abrasive paper and smooth the edges of items 13 and 14.

6 Drill ∅ 6 hole through the centre.

7 Glue and drill items 13 and 14 together.

8 Drill two holes in item 14.

9 Obtain material for pulley (item 12).

10 Using dividers, scribe the outside diameter (Fig. 1b).

11 Chain drill the turntable or use a coping saw and cut off the waste.

12 Clean up the diameter on a sanding wheel.

13 Drill ∅ 12 hole through the centre.

14 Drill a recess ∅ 20 to a depth of 5 mm.

15 Form a groove.

16 Using ∅ 20 bar, face it to a length of 25 mm on a lathe (Fig. 1c).

Item	Name	Material	Size (mm)	Quantity
1	Base	Jelutong	300 × 150 × 10	1
2	Motor support block	Jelutong	50 × 30 × 20	1
3	Motor	Bought from model shop	4½ V	1
4	Clip	Mild steel	150 × 10 × 20 swg	1
5	Bracket (for battery)	Mild steel	60 × 10 × 20 swg	2
6	Bracket (for motor)	Mild steel	70 × 10 × 20 swg	1
7	Screws	Bought out	To suit	7
8	Drawing pins	Any	Any	As necessary
9	Rheostat	Card	250 × 50	1
10	Rheostat	Fuse wire	400 mm × 1 amp	1
11	Belt	Elastic	To suit	1
12	Pulley	Jelutong	∅ 140 × 15	1
13	Pivot support block	Plastic	30 × 30 × 6	5
14	Support block base	Plastic	70 × 40 × 6	1
15	Pivot rod	Mild steel	∅ 6 × 45	1
16	Bearing insert	Aluminium	∅ 20 × 25	1
17	Leads	Cable	To suit	–
18	Probe	Brass	∅ 3 × 100	1
19	Pulley	Bought from model shop		
20	Case	Lid from scrap saucepan		1

17 Turn ∅ 12 × 20.

18 Centre drill and drill ∅ 6 to depths of 6 mm and 12 mm.

19 Cut and plane the motor support to size (Fig. 1d).

20 Drill a hole to suit the size of the motor.

21 Cut and fit two brackets (Figs 1e and h).

22 Bend brackets.

23 Mark out and file a motor clip to size (Fig. 1e).

24 Bend the clip.

25 Solder leads to the motor and to paper clips. (See brief 10.5 for soldering.)

26 Cut fuse wire to length and make a rheostat. (See note below.)

27 Cut and file the pivot rod to length, file the chamfer (Fig. 1f).

28 Make a motor-retaining clip (Fig. 1g).

29 Make and connect the probe (Fig. 1h).

30 Assemble these items on to base.

NOTE

Glueing plastic. A recommended adhesive for plastic is Tensol No. 7, but ensure that safety standards are maintained, as a well-ventilated area is necessary because of the toxic (poisonous) fumes given off.

NOTE

Rheostat. When a motor is included in the circuit, a rheostat can be made from card and fuse wire. Wrap the fuse wire around and along the length of the card and connect one end into the circuit of the roulette wheel. The probe is then touched on to the wire at intervals along the card. The motor speed will vary because of the increased electrical resistance that has been introduced.

You can purchase a rheostat or potentiometer from your local electrical/radio shop. This will give a better result, but it is more fun making your own and proving that it works!

To make a rheostat for a lamp source, another method of increasing resistance is necessary. Refer to brief 5.6.

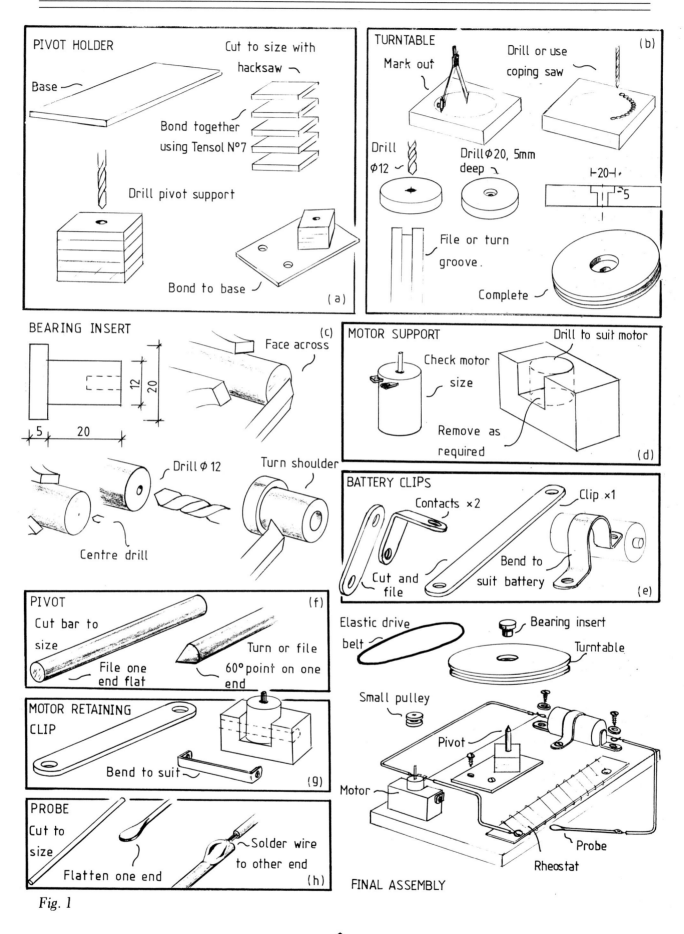

Fig. 1